WHAT'S NEW AT THE ZOO, KANGAROO?

by
Linda Diebert
and
Andra Tremper

illustrated by Roni Lavine

GOOD APPLE, INC.
Box 299
Carthage, IL 62321-0299

Copyright © Good Apple, Inc., 1982

ISBN No. 0-86653-083-5

Printing No. 9 8 7 6 5 4 3 2 1

GOOD APPLE, INC.
BOX 299
CARTHAGE, IL 62321-0299

What's New at the Zoo, Kangaroo?

Zoo +

History of the zoo, background information on zoo personnel, vocabulary list, work sheets and general activities to increase children's knowledge of a zoo.

Magnificent Mammals

MAMMALS * background information, vocabulary list, children's book list, activities and work sheets.

Awesome Avians

BIRDS * background information, vocabulary list, children's book list, activities and work sheets.

Happy Herps

REPTILES * background information, vocabulary list, children's book list, activities and work sheets.

Environmental Encounters

CONSERVATION AND ECOLOGY * background information, vocabulary list, children's book list, activities, puppet show.

Racy Resources

ADULT INFORMATION * book list, magazines, records, agency contacts and information for teaching materials.

This book was written because we believe that the zoo is no longer just a menagerie of animals, but is a marvelous living laboratory for educational experiences. Zoos provide an atmosphere for important interaction between children and animals.

We have tried to offer a wide variety of "hands-on" activities that will help adults and children learn together about wildlife. The experiences in this book allow children to become an active part of the learning process, to learn by doing.

WHAT'S NEW AT THE ZOO, KANGAROO? is meant for families, teachers or for any adult who sees the importance of instilling an appreciation of wildlife in children. It is written to promote an understanding of our world and its wildlife, but above all, to instill the idea that learning can be fun.

We hope that the information and activities provided here will help to develop a commitment to the zoo and its wildlife programs.

Going to the zoo is not simply the end of a study unit on animals, but the beginning of a concern for all living creatures.

Our thanks go to the following people who helped to make this book possible: our families and most especially our children who grew in spite of all this; Dr. Paul Chaffee and his staff at the Roeding Park Zoo; Dr. Roger LaJeunesse and Dr. Richard Haas at California State University at Fresno.

Our special gratitude to Dr. Sherman Rosenfeld for many hours of brainstorming.

There ARE MORE intelligent things to do for us PANDAS, AREN'T there?

ORIGIN OF ZOOS

Man has been fascinated with animals since the beginning of time. Pictures of wild animals have been found in caves in Lascaux, France, and are believed to be at least 25,000 years old. In China, during the 12th century B.C., the first ruler of the Chow dynasty kept a large collection of wild animals. He named this place Ling-Yu which means park of intelligence.

The word *zoo* comes from zoological garden or animal garden. The first zoo to be established as a "scientific" institution was the London Zoo with the formation of the Zoological Society of London in the late 1820's. The first zoo in the United States was established in Philadelphia in 1859.

Since World War II there has been an important and dramatic change in the purpose of a zoo. At one time, zoos were considered to be nothing more than large collections of animals displayed in rows of tiny cages. The zoo of today is vitally concerned with conserving wildlife, preserving the habitat of all wild animals, reproducing endangered species in captivity, and educating the public. Zoos now have the potential to become one of our greatest resources for learning.

NO FEEDING POLICY

Most zoos maintain a *no feeding* policy. This applies to all animals, large and small. It would be enjoyable to feed the animals, but uncontrolled feeding can actually cause harm to the animals.

Overfeeding can cause dietary deficiencies, illness and even death. Diseases can also be passed from man to animal by way of food. Just think--if each person fed only one peanut to a monkey, and 1000 people visited the zoo in a single day, what a stomachache the monkey would have! Zoo officials want their animals to remain in good health with a balanced diet that is prepared at the zoo. The food is of the very best quality and the zoo keepers know what kind of food each animal requires in order to remain trim and in good health.

So, help your local zoo by respecting their *no feeding* policy. If you are uncertain of the policy, ask at the entrance or call the zoo office.

The zoo is a world of many exciting animals, but it is also a world of zoo people. The zoo people all play an important part in maintaining a healthy and happy environment for all the zoo animals and for the people who come to visit them. The following job descriptions can be used as a part of a previsit study so that the children are familiar with the operations of a zoo. If you should happen to see any of the zoo people during your visit, be certain to stop and talk with them and give the children an opportunity to ask questions. Check with your local zoo office about arranging for special tours or talks that might be available to groups.

Zoo Director

The director makes sure the business of the zoo runs smoothly. Directors plan and design habitats that are built for each new animal. The director must be aware of the animals' needs so that the habitat has the proper wetness or dryness, places to run, climb or whatever the animals need. Directors decide which animals their zoo should have, and they make all the arrangements with other zoos or dealers. Feeding programs for all the animals are often supervised by him. The zoo director is in charge of the zoo and supervises the work of all the other people who work at the zoo.

What else does a turkey vulture need? Water, Fresh Carrion

Zoo Director

Hello — I'm Ron — Curator of Reptiles.

Zoo Curator

A curator assists the director in the supervision and development of the zoo. Each curator is an expert in the care of a particular group of animals such as birds, reptiles, and primates and they also assist the zoo keepers in maintaining the health of the animals to encourage reproduction. Curators also assist in public relations and correspondence. Most of the work on educational materials is done by the curator, and many often make presentations at local schools.

Zoo Animal Keepers

Those zoo personnel who spend the most time with the animals are the keepers. They feed and clean the animals. The keepers must know the different animals' diets and the amount of food required by each animal. The keepers' most important job is to watch every animal every day and to study closely the normal behavior and to report changes in feeding habits, symptoms of illness, signs of injury, evidence of breeding, nesting and fighting incidents to the zoo director. In addition to keeping the animals clean, the zoo keeper must also keep the homes and habitats of the animals clean and in good condition.

Zoo Veterinarian

To help keep the animals healthy, every zoo needs a veterinarian. A specialist in treating wild animals for injuries and disease, the veterinarian works with the zoo curator and keepers to determine what is wrong when an animal seems to be behaving in an unusual manner. The "vet" also checks each new animal to make certain that it is healthy before it moves in with the other animals. Each animal also receives regular vaccinations. Some zoos have their own hospitals. Other zoos take their animals to a local veterinary clinic for special needs such as x-rays.

Nursery Technician

Many zoos have a special place where baby animals can be taken care of. This is necessary when a mother is not able to care for her young. Some baby animals also may be injured or may be too small and need special attention. Nursery attendants give all the baby animals the special care and feeding they may require. They also assist the other zoo keepers whenever and wherever they are needed.

Night Zoo Attendant

This zoo person helps to maintain security at the zoo during closing hours and is also involved with janitorial and cleaning tasks within zoo buildings and the grounds area. The night attendant helps with rodent and pest control and may also be involved in some of the feeding of the animals.

Grounds Keeper

The grounds keeper plants and cares for the lawns, the trees and the plants in the zoo. He only takes care of grounds that are outside the enclosures. It is the job of the animal keepers to care for the plants within the cages. The grounds keeper also helps to provide security for the zoo and the animals and provides information at the request of the visitors.

Vocabulary

adaptation:	A genetically determined characteristic that enhances the ability of an animal to cope with its environment.
browser:	Animals that eat shoots, twigs and the leaves of trees and shrubs.
camouflage:	To disguise one's self in order not to be seen.
captivity:	Kept in confinement as in a zoo.
carnivore:	Eats meat only.
diurnal:	Active by day.
gestation:	Period of time from conception to birth.
grazer:	Animal that feeds on low herbage such as grass and weeds.
habitat:	Natural dwelling place of an animal.
herbivore:	Animal that eats plants.
hibernation:	Winter sleep-inactive during cold weather.
niche:	An animal's specific function within its habitat.
nocturnal:	Active by night.
omnivore:	Eats both meat and plants.
predator:	An animal that preys on other animals for food.
prey:	Animals that are hunted by other animals.
territory:	Area established by an animal for food gathering, breeding or nesting.

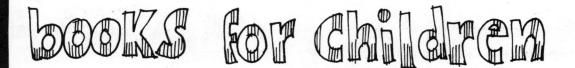

books for children

Bridges, William, *Zoo Babies,* Morrow Press.
Carle, Eric, *1, 2, 3, to the Zoo,* World Press.
Colonius, Lillian, *At the Zoo,* Melmont Publishers.
Geisel, T.S., *If I Ran the Zoo,* Random House.
Gray, Zhenya, *Who Is It,* Viking Press.
Green, Carla, *Animal Doctors: What They Do,* Harper & Row.
Hader, Berta, *Lost in the Zoo,* Macmillan.
Hewett, Joan, *Watching Them Grow: Inside a Zoo Nursery,* Little, Brown.
Hirschmann, Linda, *In a Lick of a Flick of a Tongue,* Dodd, Mead & Company.
Ipcar, Dahlov, *Wild and Tame Animals,* Doubleday.
Lewis, Stephen, *Zoo City,* Greenwillow Books.
Marietta, Marcia, *Zoo in Her Bed,* Coward-McCann.
McGovern, Ann, *Zoo Where Are You?* Harper & Row.
McNaught, Harry, *Animal Babies,* Random House.
Meeks, Esther, *Something New at the Zoo,* Follett Press.

Zoo animal diets

Zoo it

Since the foods animals eat in their natural habitat are not always available at the zoo, suitable substitutions must be found. The zoo director works very closely with the curators and keepers to develop a proper diet for each animal. Below are examples of food used by various zoos. Not every zoo will use the exact items listed here.

animal	Food — wild	Food — captivity
Leopard Lion Cheetah (carnivore) Tiger	Wild animals such as deer, zebra, antelope, and wild pigs.	Commercial diets such as Zupreem--a specially prepared formula of meat, bone meal, blood, cereal products and vitamins.
Antelope Deer (herbivore) Zebra Bison	Grass, leaves, weeds, salt lick (natural)	Alfalfa, grain pellets, pressed hay cubes, fresh hydroponically grown barley
Seal (carnivore) Sea Lion	Live, whole fish	Whole, frozen fish such as mackerel, smelt. Fish are fortified with salt and thiamine
Bear (omnivore)	Ants, grubs, fish, dead animals, and berries.	Omnivore chow (a biscuit similar to dog food), fruits and meat supplements
Elephant (herbivore)	Banana plants, grass, leaves, great quantities of water	Hay, alfalfa, pressed hay cubes, fresh hydroponic grown barley.
Snake (carnivore)	Mice, rats, gophers, frogs, small birds, other snakes, fish.	Most snakes: mice Garter snakes: goldfish Pythons/large snakes: rats, rabbits, chickens
Tortoise (herbivore)	Leaves, grass and fruit	Chopped spinach, carrots, apples, Bermuda and other grasses, tricalcium phosphate for a hard shell
Hawk Eagle (carnivore) Owl	Small birds, mammals and reptiles	Birds of Prey Diet--consists of ground meat, cereal and bone meal. Occasional live or freshly killed animals
Gorilla Orangutan (omnivore) Chimpanzee	Fruits, leaves, roots and other vegetable material	Fruits and vegetables and occasionally a meat supplement

An important part of the zoo operation is the designing of an exhibit or habitat to fit the needs of the animal being displayed.

While at the zoo, children should be encouraged to observe the animal's space and how the animal lives in this space. Use the Design a Zoo work sheet to help with this observation. After the children have visited the zoo and completed their work sheets, divide them into teams for the following activity:

Write up information cards for each team. The cards should list specific animal needs and habits. Each team must design and draw a picture of its planned animal environment according to the needs listed on their cards. Teams then report back to the class for .evaluation by everyone. Further development of this activity can include building scale models of each environment.

Suggestions for activity cards:

1. This is a large mammal that likes to swim, eat fish and sunbathe. Salt water must be available for its eyes and skin.
2. This is an animal that lives in a family group, needs to burrow and tunnel and likes to eat fruits and vegetables.
3. This animal needs an area for sun protection, soft dirt to dig in and lay eggs, and a source of heat in the winter. It likes to eat grass, fruits and vegetables.
4. This animal is a large tree-dwelling mammal that needs shelter from the cold and a large exercise area. It eats fruits, vegetables and leaves.

adopt an animal

Scientists spend a lot of time watching animals. They do this to learn about what the animal eats, where it lives and how it relates to others of its own kind.

Since the zoo is a very exciting and distracting place for children, it is sometimes hard for them to focus on what the animals are doing. Use the Adopt an Animal checklist found in the back of this chapter to help children observe the behavior of one animal in the zoo.

*Thanks to Arlyn Christopherson, Oakland Zoo Wildlife School, for her assistance with the Adopt an Animal activity.

apron Surprise

Zoo it

Either buy or make a full-length apron. Then, using contrasting material, cut several pockets that are each eight inches square. The outside of each pocket should have a different animal on it. You can use the animal patterns found at the end of this chapter.

Sew the pockets to the front of the apron. Wear the apron while working in the classroom or at home. If the child can identify the animal on the pocket and/or relate some certain information about the animal, then he/she can be rewarded by reaching into the pocket to find a surprise. Pocket surprises could include: animal finger puppets, a book, a special poem, a treat or a privilege such as a half-hour of free time.

animal antics

You will need three yards of heavy material such as canvas or corduroy to make the playing board and pieces of contrasting material or felt to make circles. Cut eight-inch circles and attach in a random fashion to the three yards of material. Use the animal patterns found at the end of this chapter for the animal pictures.

Cut out the pictures, cover with clear Con-Tact paper, and glue one inside each circle. (Or make animals out of felt and glue them inside the circles.) Make a deck of animal cards by gluing duplicate animal pictures onto heavy cardboard. Cover with Con-Tact paper.

Lay out the large piece of material. Have each child draw a card and step where his/her card tells him/her to. Variations for older children:

1. Use a different body part to touch each animal until you lose your balance.

2. An adult or another child draws a card and describes the animal or a characteristic of the animal. For example, put your left foot on the animal that eats fish, step on the animal that is carnivorous, put your right hand on a mammal, etc.

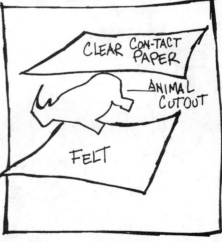

CLEAR CON-TACT PAPER

ANIMAL CUTOUT

FELT

animal sounds

ARF

SSS

zoo it

CAW

OWWWW

Discuss the animal sounds that were heard at the zoo. Talk about the loud sounds, soft sounds, etc. Now help the children transfer these sounds to movement. For example, a roar might be interpreted as a bold, swishing movement; a grunt might be a quick, jerky movement; the chattering of monkeys might inspire the children to do some silly running or jumping; a barking seal might sound like quick jumps and a hissing snake might be interpreted as slow, low-to-the-ground movement.

You can also use musical instruments to expand the discussion on sound. A drum may sound like a lion's roar or an elephant's footsteps. Bells or a triangle may sound like singing birds or chattering monkeys. Use musical instruments to keep time to chants about animals.

Example:

Snakes are crawling, crawling, crawling
Snakes are crawling on the ground.   (slowly)

Monkeys are chattering, chattering, chattering
Monkeys are chattering all around.   (faster)

Lions are roaring, roaring, roaring
Lions are roaring all day long.   (beat drums)

Birds are singing, singing, singing
Birds are singing a beautiful song. (Use triangle or bell)

Sound Safari

People rely heavily on sight to obtain information about their environments. This activity will enable your children to use another sense and focus on a different aspect of the zoo.

While on a visit to the zoo, stop at several different locations throughout the zoo. Have the children stand quietly and listen. Count and classify the sounds that are heard and ask the following questions: Were the sounds made by animals, people or machines? Were they loud or soft sounds? Was there a pattern or rhythm to the sound? Try going on a sound safari on the school playground, in the home or around the neighborhood.

Footprint Frolic

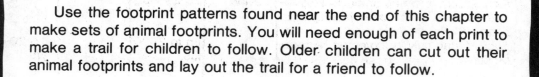

Use the footprint patterns found near the end of this chapter to make sets of animal footprints. You will need enough of each print to make a trail for children to follow. Older children can cut out their animal footprints and lay out the trail for a friend to follow.

Set up animal trails and place a picture of the correct animal at the end of each trail. Hand out sample footprints to match the trails you have set up. Let each child find his/her trail and follow it to discover the animal that matches the footprint. Once children understand the game, it can be left out for learning stations or small-group play. Younger children can pretend to be the animal as they follow the footprints. Cover footprints with clear Con-Tact paper so that they can be used again.

Baby Babble

Many animals have different names while they are young. Use the names listed below for the activity that follows:

Cub - bear/lion/tiger	Joey - kangaroo
Calf - bison/elephant/giraffe	Pup - seal
Kit - fox	Lamb - sheep
Kid - goat	Cygnet - swan
Gosling - goose	Foal - zebra

Divide children into two groups and form two lines facing each other. One group will be adult animals and one group will be the baby animals. Give each group member a color-coded card with the name of an animal on it. (Pictures can be used for nonreaders.) Help each person to read his card or look at the picture and then have him decide what sound his animal makes. At the proper signal, all team members move forward making their own special sounds. When babies and adults have found each other, they can check themselves by matching the colors on their cards.

Cub

Fawn

Cygnet

Bear

Deer

Swan

Nursery News

adult / baby name	did you know?	ave. wt. birth	adult	ave. # born	ave. life-span
ANTEATER	Mother carries young on back, they remain together until mother is pregnant again	3 lbs.	23-29 lbs.	1	10-14 yrs.
AMERICAN BISON/CALF	Today found only in protected herds in parks		up to 2400 lbs.	1	15-20 yrs.
BALD EAGLE/EAGLET	Considered to be a rare bird, is also our national symbol	4-5 oz.	10 lbs.	2-3 eggs	10 years
CAMEL/CALF	Can go as much as a week without water	100 lbs.	1½ tons	1	30 years or longer
CHIMPANZEE	Perhaps the most intelligent primate next to man	4½ lbs.	90-150 lbs.	1	30-50 yrs.
ELEPHANT/CALF	Largest land mammal	150 lbs.	3½ tons	1	60-70 yrs.
GIRAFFE/CALF	Tallest animal, can run as fast as 29 mph.	125 lbs.	1-2 tons	1	15-20 yrs.
GORILLA	Rarest of man-like apes, no natural enemies except for man	4½ lbs.	300-600 lbs.	1	35-40 yrs.
HIPPOPOTAMUS/ CALF	Give birth to young underwater, nurse young underwater	60 lbs.	3-4 tons	1	30-35 yrs.
LION/CUB	Females do the hunting for the pride	2-3 lbs.	300-400 lbs.	2-3	20 yrs. or more
LLAMA	Capable of carrying loads weighing as much as 200 lbs.		300 lbs.	1	20 yrs.
SPIDER MONKEY	Prehensile tail serves as a fifth arm or leg		13-17 lbs.	1	10-15 yrs.
ORANGUTAN	Rarest of the apes	3 lbs.	100-200 lbs.	1	35-40 yrs.
OSTRICH/CHICK	Only two toes, this bird can run as fast as 35 mph	3-4 lbs.	300 lbs.	30 eggs/yr.	20 yrs.
POLAR BEAR/CUB	Has fur around footpads to prevent slipping on ice.	1½ lbs.	1000 lbs.	1 in first litter; then 2	30 yrs.
RHINOCEROS/ CALF	Very poor eyesight, can run as fast as 30 mph	150-180 lbs.	4 tons	1	30 yrs.
SEA LION/PUP	Only seals that can be trained to perform	10-12 lbs.	300-600 lbs.	1	20 yrs.
TIGER/CUB	Good swimmers	2-3 lbs.	250-425 lbs.	2-3	18-20 yrs.
WALLAROO/JOEY	Tail acts as a balancer	1 gram	50 lbs.	1	15-20 yrs.
ZEBRA/FOAL	Can run as fast as 40 mph	56 lbs.	700 lbs.	1	20-30 yrs.

This activity should be done after a trip to the zoo. This can be done as a group activity where the children listen to the description and give their answers orally. Older children can work on the activity individually and write their responses down on a work sheet. Older children can also reverse the procedure. Give them an animal and have them describe the type of habitat that animal lives in at the zoo you visited. You will have to make up your cage descriptions according to what is available at the zoo in your area. Here are some examples.

These animals live on an island with water all the way around it. There is a door going inside the island where the animals sleep. Some of the animals hide in a tall palm tree on the island. These playful animals swing on a big wheel and climb chains. WHO LIVES HERE? (spider monkeys, squirrel monkeys)

This exhibit is a big tall cage with trees growing through the roof. The animals that live there perch on rocks and bushes around clean, white pools. A stairway goes all the way around this cage for people to walk on. There are nest boxes at the top of the cage for the animals to use. All the animals here eat meat. WHO LIVES HERE? (birds of prey - hawks, eagles, owls)

In the middle of this exhibit is a deep, blue pool. There is one tree on a little island that shades the pool. The animals here swim well and have a tunnel to swim through. There is a water slide for the animals to play on. This area smells like fish. WHO LIVES HERE? (seals, sea lions)

zoo bag

Learning is enhanced when all of the senses are used. Imagine how exciting it would be to hold an ostrich egg while observing the behavior of a *real live* ostrich or to touch a porcupine quill while watching a porcupine. Props like these can be carried with you to improve the quality of the zoo visit experience.

You will also need a tote bag to hold the props, preferably one with a shoulder strap to make it easier to carry. Below is a list of possible things to include in your zoo bag. Many (like the feathers and snake sheddings) can be obtained at your local zoo.

binoculars - for a closer look at distant animals
bird and reptile eggs
flash cards - containing the names of animals
musical instruments - to use in singing a song to a
    monkey. Watch what he does.

porcupine quills
bird calls
feathers
small hand mirrors
samples of animal food
skulls, teeth and horns

Pictures of animals can show some type of behavior you can't observe in the zoo such as courtship or camouflage. Pictures can also show close-up animal features that can't easily be seen, such as scales on the back of an alligator.

5-line rhyme

Poetry is an excellent medium for communicating feelings about animals. Poetry can also be used to help sharpen observation skills. Below is a form for a simple five-line animal poem. Older students can choose animals and create their own poems. Younger children or those who can't read can create an animal poem as a group project.

Line One--Name of the animal
Line Two--Two words that describe what the animal looks, feels or sounds like
Line Three--Three words that tell how it moves or something the animal does
Line Four--Four words that give a thought about the animal
Line Five--Repeat the name of the animal

Example: Tiger
    Sinuous stripes
    Almond eyes shining
    Silent form moving in the twilight
    Tiger

Adopt an Animal

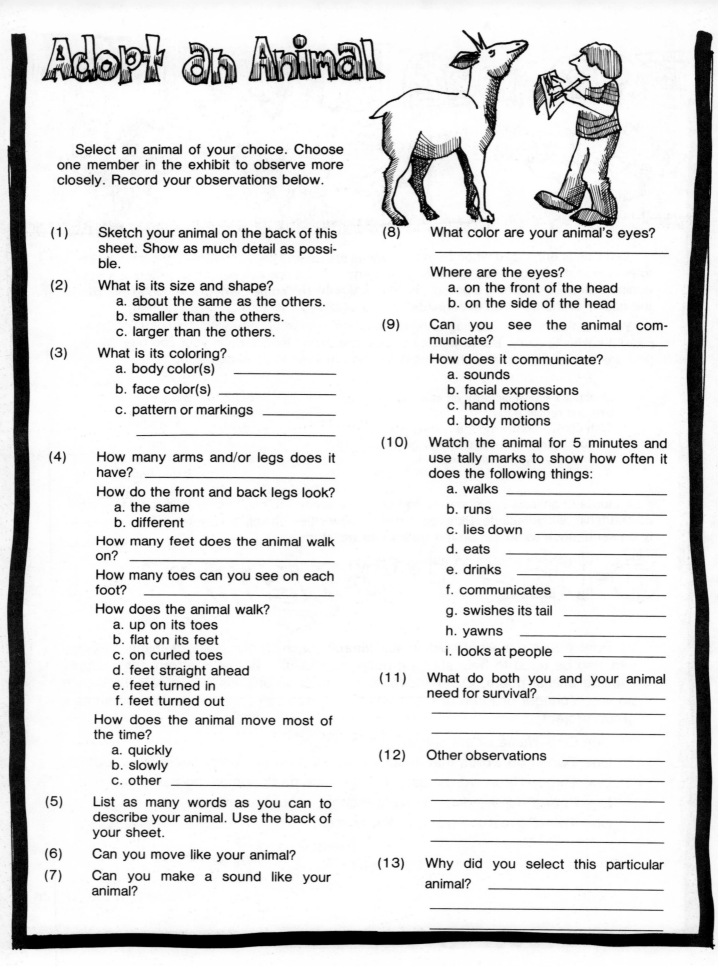

Select an animal of your choice. Choose one member in the exhibit to observe more closely. Record your observations below.

(1) Sketch your animal on the back of this sheet. Show as much detail as possible.

(2) What is its size and shape?
   a. about the same as the others.
   b. smaller than the others.
   c. larger than the others.

(3) What is its coloring?
   a. body color(s) _____
   b. face color(s) _____
   c. pattern or markings _____
   _____

(4) How many arms and/or legs does it have? _____

   How do the front and back legs look?
   a. the same
   b. different

   How many feet does the animal walk on? _____

   How many toes can you see on each foot? _____

   How does the animal walk?
   a. up on its toes
   b. flat on its feet
   c. on curled toes
   d. feet straight ahead
   e. feet turned in
   f. feet turned out

   How does the animal move most of the time?
   a. quickly
   b. slowly
   c. other _____

(5) List as many words as you can to describe your animal. Use the back of your sheet.

(6) Can you move like your animal?

(7) Can you make a sound like your animal?

(8) What color are your animal's eyes?
   _____

   Where are the eyes?
   a. on the front of the head
   b. on the side of the head

(9) Can you see the animal communicate? _____

   How does it communicate?
   a. sounds
   b. facial expressions
   c. hand motions
   d. body motions

(10) Watch the animal for 5 minutes and use tally marks to show how often it does the following things:
   a. walks _____
   b. runs _____
   c. lies down _____
   d. eats _____
   e. drinks _____
   f. communicates _____
   g. swishes its tail _____
   h. yawns _____
   i. looks at people _____

(11) What do both you and your animal need for survival? _____
   _____
   _____

(12) Other observations _____
   _____
   _____
   _____
   _____

(13) Why did you select this particular animal? _____
   _____
   _____

14

When "zoo people" design animal exhibits they must consider all the animal's needs. Use the form below to help you observe the exhibit of an animal.

Animal's name _____

(1)   Is there drinking water? _____

(2)   Where is the water?
        in a pool   in a dish   in a sprinkler

(3)   Is there shelter for the animal? _____

(4)   What does the shelter look like?
        a cave   a tree   a log
        other _____

(5)   Is the exhibit large enough for the animal to exercise? _____

(6)   Are there places for the animal to:
        climb   swim
        run   fly
        dig   rest

(7)   Is there a place for the animal to sleep? _____
        What does this sleeping area look like? _____
        _____
        _____

(8)   How does the zoo keeper feed and care for the animal? _____
        _____
        _____

(9)   Do you like the way the exhibit looks? _____
        Why? _____
        _____

(10)   How would you change this exhibit? _____
        _____
        _____

african elephant

black rhinoceros

malayan tapir

flamingo

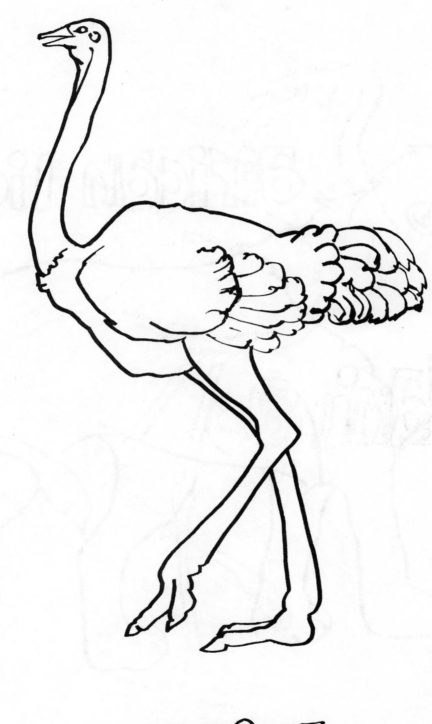

ostrich

red Kangaroo

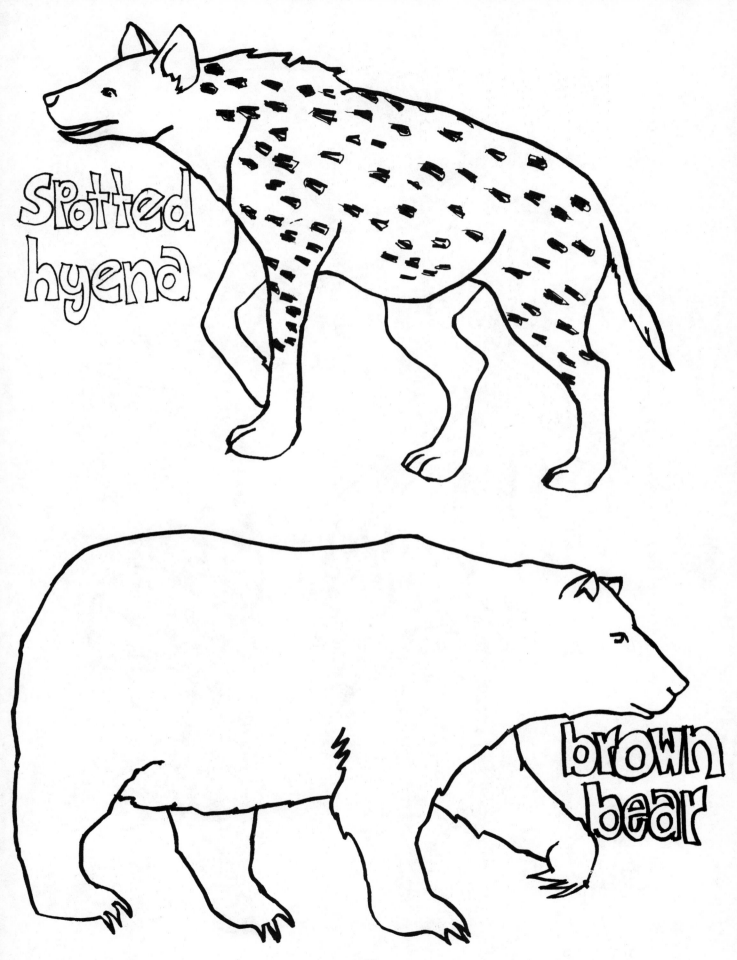

Spotted hyena

brown bear

crocodile

zebra

Footprint Frolic

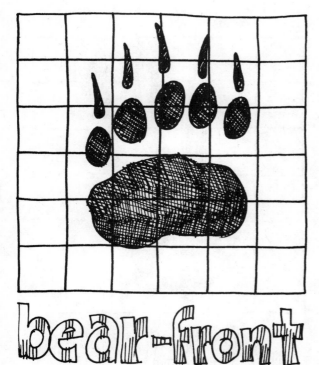

bear-front

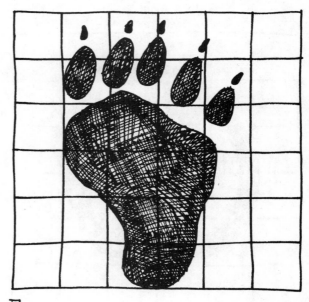

bear-rear

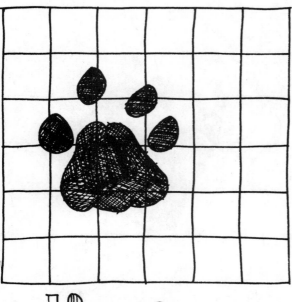

lion

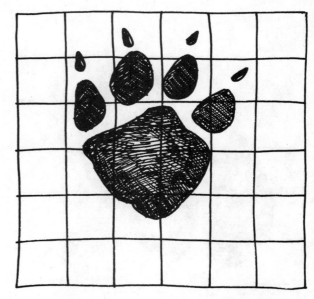

hyena

Footprint Frolic

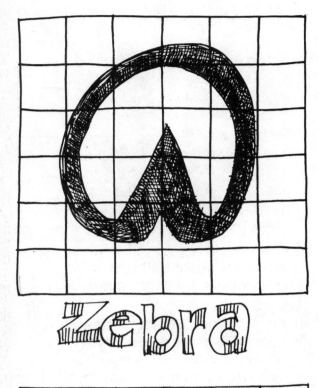

Zebra

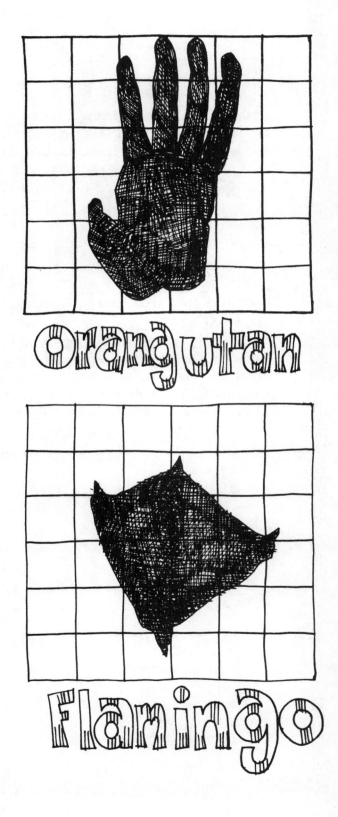

Orangutan

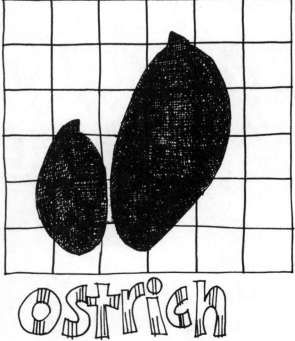

Ostrich

Flamingo

Mammalformation

The word mammal is derived from "mama," the Latin word for breast. Mammals have several distinguishing characteristics. They nurse their young with milk secreted from the mammary glands of the female, and their skin is covered with fur or hair. In some mammals (for example, whales and elephants), hair is present on the body in the early stages of life, but most of it is lost in adulthood.

Mammals are found throughout the world. They maintain a constant body temperature, regardless of environmental conditions, and this "warm-bloodedness" has allowed them to inhabit climates too cold for reptiles or amphibians. This consistency of body temperature also helps to make mammals more active and energetic.

Almost all mammals have teeth. The size and shape of each type of tooth is related to the diet of the particular animal. Carnivores have enlarged canine teeth for stabbing prey (lion, tiger). Rodents have evergrowing incisor teeth for gnawing (prairie dog, squirrel).

Even when they are normally active, mammals need periods of rest or sleep. Elephants rest in short naps which last only a few minutes. The more normal pattern for rest in mammals is one or two extended periods of inactivity during a twenty-four hour period. Animals that are active during the day are termed diurnal. Those that are active at night and sleep during the day are termed nocturnal.

Divided into seventeen different orders, there are 4,000 kinds of mammals. Below you will find a list of some unusual mammals and some interesting information about them.

Bats	only mammal that can fly
Duckbill platypus	egg laying mammals, after young hatch they lap
Spiny anteater	milk which comes from the mammary glands - found only in Australia
African elephant	largest land mammal
Blue whale	largest water mammal
Pigmy shrew	smallest mammal
Giant anteater	has no teeth

The Nursery News chart found in the Zoo It chapter also lists several kinds of mammals.

Vocabulary

antlers:	Bony growth on the head of some male hooved animals, shed annually.
canine:	Member of the dog family.
feline:	Member of the cat family.
gestation:	Carrying of young before birth; pregnancy.
herd:	Social group in which hooved animals live.
horns:	Bony growth on the head of a mammal that is not shed and is covered with cuticle covering.
in velvet:	Soft covering of antlers in the early stages of growth.
marsupial:	Pouched animals, the young live and develop after they are born in the pouch which is on the outside of the stomach as in kangaroos and opossums.
prehensile:	Able to grasp or hold as the tail of a spider monkey, and hands of apes.
pride:	Family or group of lions that live together.
primate:	An order of mammals including monkeys, apes and man.
ruminant:	Cud chewing as in cows and camels.
shed:	Loss of old hair, fur, skin or antlers which are replaced with new growth.
warm-blooded:	Body temperature stays even most of the time.

books for Children

Carle, Eric, and Fisher, Aileen, *Do Bears Have Mothers, Too?* Thomas V. Crowell Co.

Davidson, Margaret, *Wild Animal Families,* Hastings House.

Day, Jennifer, *What Is a Mammal?* Golden Press.

Fatio, Louise, *Happy Lions,* McGraw Hill.

Fields, Alice, *Seals,* Watts Publishing.

Freschet, Bernice, *Grizzly Bear,* Thomas Y. Crowell Co.

Freschet, Bernice, *The Happy Dromedary,* Thomas Y. Crowell Co.

Hogner, Dorothy Childs, *Sea Mammals,* Thomas Y. Crowell Co.

Hunt, Joyce, and Selsam, Millicent, *A First Look at Whales,* Walker & Co.

Kishida, Eriko, *Hippopotamus,* Prentice-Hall.

Lavine, Sigmund and Scuro, Vincent, *Wonders of Elephants,* Dodd-Mead.

McGovern, Ann, *Great Gorillas,* Scholastic Book Services.

Michel, Anna, *Little Wild Chimpanzee,* Random House.

Morris, Robert, *Dolphin,* Harper & Row.

Palmer, Helen, *I Was Kissed by a Seal at the Zoo,* Random House.

Pluckrose, Henery, *Apes,* Gloucester Press.

Pluckrose, Henery, *Lions and Tigers,* Gloucester Press.

Preston, Edna, *Monkey in the Jungle,* Viking Press.

Schlein, Miriam, *A Lucky Porcupine,* Four Winds Press.

adapt-a-body

Many animals have special body adaptations which help them survive in their environments. Children can better understand adaptation by looking at specific animals and comparing their own bodies to these animals.

Use the equipment listed below to help your children adapt their bodies to desert or aquatic life. You can give the children a list of the animal adaptations and let them choose the right equipment to adapt their own bodies. This can also be done as a group activity where one child is dressed with the special equipment as the whole group discusses each adaptation.

Desert Life (Camel)

Animal Adaptation	Equipment for Human Adaptation
Well-developed muscles around the nostrils can close nostrils to keep sand from coming in.	Nose plugs
Double, long eyelashes to protect against sand and sun.	Sunglasses, goggles
Broad, flat feet with undivided soles for sand travel.	Snow shoes
Able to store water in tissues so that they can go long periods without water.	Water container to carry

Aquatic Life (Sea Lion)

Limbs modified into flippers for swimming.	Swim fins
Thick layers of blubber beneath the skin provide insulation and buoyancy.	Wet suit, coat, life jacket
Ability to store large amounts of oxygen in the muscle tissues.	Snorkel or a replica of a diving tank

Believe it or not people are mammals, too! We are warm-blooded, we have hair, and we can nurse our babies with milk. Like other mammals we have had to adapt to our environment. The following activities will help children understand mammals a little more:

1. Ask the children to draw a picture of themselves. After the picture is complete, have them look at the eyes, feet, and hands in the picture. Ask, "How do your eyes, feet, and hands help you to live?" On the same piece of paper, ask children to complete these sentences:

My eyes help me _____.

My feet help me _____.

My hands help me _____.

Explain that people's eyes, hands, and feet are adaptations that help them to live.

Next, discuss with the children the way in which they adapt their behavior to meet different situations. Some questions you might ask: Was it hot or cold when we came to school this morning? How did you adapt or change to go outside? Is there anything you do when you eat that has changed since you were a baby? (drink out of a glass instead of a bottle, etc.)

2. Have the class make a list of the things that all animals need to live and be healthy. They are: food, water, exercise, rest, sunshine, and a place to live. Do people need these things, too?

Stress throughout these activities that humans have large brains and that is their most important adaptation. We can use our brains to develop tools and machines to help us feed and protect ourselves. Other animals must rely on their instincts, the training they receive from their parents, and the adaptations made by their particular species.

*Thanks to Brandy Pound, Curator of Education, San Francisco Zoo, and to the San Francisco Zoological Society, for their contribution to the You Are a Mammal activity.

Yipes Stripes

One of the ways animals camouflage themselves from their enemies is to be the same color as their surroundings.

Many mammals have interesting designs or patterns on their bodies which help them to hide in tall grass or bushes. Animals in zoos are out of place. That is, they cannot blend in with their backgrounds and are easy to find.

Help your students learn more about animal coloration and camouflage by trying the following activities:

1. Make copies of the animal coloration cards found at the end of this chapter. Cut and mount each square on a piece of poster board. Cut and mount the animal name on the back of the card for self-checking. Laminate. Use the cards of the animals that can be found at your local zoo.

    At the start of your zoo tour, hand each child a pattern card. Remind the children to watch for mammals with stripes and spots. The first one to find the animal design on his card should signal the group.

2. Look at the stripes on the body of a tiger or zebra. Ask the children why the stripes run up and down instead of across the animal's body. To demonstrate the answer do the following: Draw vertical black stripes on a 4" by 5" white card. Draw horizontal black stripes on another white card. Make sure the stripes are spaced evenly on both cards. Set the cards side by side in a tall grassy area and have the students stand back away from the cards. Which set of stripes are the hardest to see? The vertical stripes should be more camouflaged.

Milk Magic

One of the defining characteristics of all mammals is that they nurse their young with milk secreted from the mammary glands of the female. Mammals and their relationship to milk can provide the framework for a unit on milk and milk products. Use the following activities and recipes to make your own "MILK MAGIC."

1. Discuss where milk comes from. Where do babies get milk? Which animals give us milk? Which animals give milk to people around the world?

   Goats - parts of Europe, Mexico, and the United States
   Donkeys - parts of China
   Reindeer - Arctic lands
   Camels - deserts of Africa and Asia
   Buffalo - India, Africa

2. Discuss and observe the differences and similarities in the varieties of milk. Encourage children to smell and taste different kinds of milk. Choose from buttermilk, whole milk, skim milk, nonfat dry milk, condensed milk, goat's milk, and evaporated milk. Similar tasting experiences can also be done with milk products - yogurt, ice cream, sour cream, whipping cream, kinds of cheeses, etc.

3. Discuss how milk is processed and how milk comes to us. How does the milk go from cows to the container? Visit a dairy farm or dairy plant.

Use the following recipes for creative cooking with your children:

Orange "Julius" Drink

1 6-oz. can orange juice concentrate
1½ cans water (use empty juice can)
1½ cans milk
2 eggs
1 teaspoon vanilla
ice cubes

Place all ingredients in a blender. Blend. Add ice to make it slushy.

Frozen Pineapple Buttermilk

1 qt. buttermilk
½ - ¾ cup honey
½ cup lemon juice
1 20 oz. can crushed pineapple
grated rind of one lemon

Measure all ingredients and mix together. Freeze in a freezer tray until almost solid. Put in a bowl and beat until light and fluffy. Return to tray at least one hour. Pour into glasses. Serves 16.

Cottage Cheese Cinnamon Toast

Raisin bread
Cinnamon
Cottage cheese

Spread cottage cheese on bread. Sprinkle cinnamon on top of cottage cheese and place on a cookie sheet. Put under the broiler until cheese melts. Cut into quarters before serving.

Yogurt Gelatin

2 tablespoons unflavored gelatin
3 cups juice (choose your favorite kind)
1 cup yogurt (make sure it blends with the juice flavor)

Mix gelatin with ¼ cup cold juice. Boil another ¼ cup of juice and add to gelatin. Stir until the gelatin has dissolved. Add yogurt and remaining juice, stir and place in refrigerator until set.

Mystery Mammals

Provide drawing paper and colored pencils. One person thinks of a mammal. Without naming it, he/she begins to describe the mammal feature by feature. The rest of the group draws each feature as it is being described. The first person to complete his drawing and guess the mammal may then select the next mystery mammal.

For example, a description of a kangaroo might sound like this... "I am thinking of a mammal with a medium-sized head, long ears, red-brown fur and a long tail which is used for balance. This mammal sits on its hind legs, eats grass and stands about five feet tall. It has a pouch on its abdomen and likes to jump very fast."

A teacher or parent working with younger children might slowly place each feature on a flannel board until the children can guess the mammal in question.

Hair and There

After reviewing the characteristics of mammals listed in the background information, take your children on a mammal search around the zoo. Use the Hair and There checklist found in the back of this chapter to see how many different things you can find out about the mammals in the zoo.

A CAMEL is A MAMMAL AND SO is A gnu. HOW MANY MAMMALS live iN the ZOO?

In this activity children must match the mammal to the continent on which it lives, the habitat in which it survives and the food it eats.

You will need four half-gallon milk cartons. Cover each with colored construction paper. Take one of the cartons and draw the outline of a different continent on each of the four sides. Write the continent name next to the drawing. On the second milk carton, draw or glue a picture of a different animal on each of the four sides. For milk carton number three, draw or glue on a picture of the various kinds of food eaten. On the last milk carton, draw or glue on pictures of the habitats of the various animals. (Old wildlife magazines are an excellent source for pictures.)

Possible combinations to be used:

CONTINENT	ANIMAL	HABITAT	DIET
Africa	Giraffe	Savannah	Leaves and grass
North America	Black-footed ferret	Prairie	Small mammals
Europe	Siberian ibex	Mountains	Grass
Australia	Platypus	Rivers, streams	Worms, Crustaceans
South America	Spider monkey	Trees	Nuts, fruits

gorilla brunch

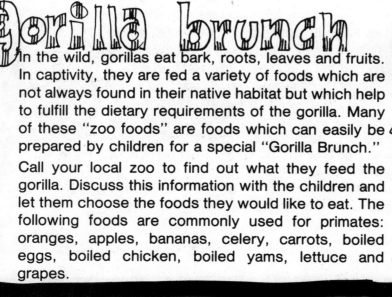

In the wild, gorillas eat bark, roots, leaves and fruits. In captivity, they are fed a variety of foods which are not always found in their native habitat but which help to fulfill the dietary requirements of the gorilla. Many of these "zoo foods" are foods which can easily be prepared by children for a special "Gorilla Brunch."

Call your local zoo to find out what they feed the gorilla. Discuss this information with the children and let them choose the foods they would like to eat. The following foods are commonly used for primates: oranges, apples, bananas, celery, carrots, boiled eggs, boiled chicken, boiled yams, lettuce and grapes.

Animals talk to each other by using various signals such as sounds, flashes of color, scent and body movement. These signals are used during courtship, when sounding an alarm, when defending territory or when threatening a less dominant member of the group.

Many examples of animal communication can be given:

1. The position of a wolf's tail can signal submission when tucked between its hind legs, or it can signal confidence when held high in the air.

2. A mother tiger will use the white marking on her ears to signal her cubs to stay with her.

3. A male bird sings a song to warn other males to stay away from his territory. He also sings to attract a female.

4. The male rhino will mark his territory with urine.

To further investigate animal communication, try the following:

a. Observe different animal signals at the zoo. Can you figure out what they are saying?

b. Review the different types of signals that people use (traffic signals, a wave, a frown, the color red used to signal danger, etc.).

c. Separate children into several groups. Hand each group a slip of paper with one of the following statements written on it: "A predator is coming," "I've found some food," "This is my territory," "I am angry," "I am afraid," "I like you," "Don't move!" "It is safe to come out now." Each group must work together to create their own signal to represent the statement. No words may be used. After the signal is agreed upon, the children can then demonstrate the signal. The others must then watch and see if they can guess what is being said.

Fingers and Thumbs

Materials: one peanut per child
masking tape

Activity: Divide students into four groups. Let students help each other tape their hands in the following manner.

GROUP 1   tapes hands so that neither fingers nor thumbs can move freely.

GROUP 2   tapes thumbs to the palms of their hands so that their fingers move but their thumbs do not.

GROUP 3   team members tape thumbs to the sides of their hands so that only the top joint of the thumb can move and the fingers are free.

GROUP 4   team members can help others with taping, but their hands are not taped at all.

Ask each student to shell and eat one peanut using his taped hands. You may time each group to see who finishes first, or you may just want them to explore their limited ability with other objects like pencils. GROUP 4 members can tape their hands as they wish for this activity.

When the activity is complete, tell students which animals have hands similar to their own "taped predicaments."

GROUP 1: Hands like those of a bear. A bear would roll the peanut on the ground to break the shell and then pick up the meat with his tongue.

GROUP 2: Hands like those of a spider monkey. These monkeys have no thumbs at all to get in their way as they swing through the trees so they merely crack the peanut with their teeth.

GROUP 3: Hands like a chimpanzee with the limited use of very short thumbs. The chimp often scoops up food with a cupped hand.

GROUP 4: Untaped hands have the same sort of mobility experienced by members of the baboon family, although humans do have slightly longer and more dexterous thumbs.

Ask your students if they think fingers and thumbs are really all that important. Tell them that the hand is an important tool for many animals, but not for all. Does the giraffe have thumbs? No, but he has a long prehensile tongue to help in feeding. Discuss adaptations of other animals that don't have fingers and thumbs. Further study on adaptations can be done with the People Are Animals activity found in this chapter.

*Thanks to Brandy Pound, Curator of Education, San Francisco Zoo, and to the San Francisco Zoological Society for the Fingers and Thumbs activity.

big foot

Big Foot in California, Sasquatch in Canada and the Abominable Snowman in Napal are all names that have been used to describe a large, ape-like mammal that walks upright. Many people in different areas of the world have claimed to have seen this animal. Is there really such a creature? Although there have been many accounts recorded by witnesses, casts of footprints and photographs, scientists have never examined an actual specimen of any kind. Big Foot supposedly stands over eight feet tall, weighs 600-700 pounds and has a foot that measures seventeen inches in length. Explore these possibilities with your children:

1. Without showing your students a photograph of Big Foot, have them draw a picture of what they think he must really look like.

2. Measure off the animal's height on the wall.
    Then compare it with the height of an adult and a young human being. What would an animal of this size eat? Where would it probably live? Compare it to existing mammals children know of today.

3. Provide books and articles on Big Foot. Allow time for students to research the topic. Split the group into two teams for a debate.
    Team One takes the position that Big Foot is real.
    Team Two takes the position that Big Foot is a myth.

4. Write a story or newspaper article about Big Foot. Have the children imagine that they have just met the animal face to face. What would they do? What would they tell everyone else about the experience?

hooves and horns

A complete zoo experience should include the opportunity to examine the animals closely to discover their special body adaptations. Use the Hooves and Horns work sheet found in the back of this chapter to help children look at specific animal body parts. Younger children can simply check off the part as they see it. Older children can identify the animal and make notes about the specific purpose or adaptation of the body part. The correct name for each corresponding animal is listed below:

1. bison
2. deer
3. pronghorn antelope
4. gazelle
5. ram
6. rhino
7. beaver
8. monkey
9. giraffe
10. coyote
11. jaguar
12. raccoon
13. zebra
14. gazelle
15. camel
16. elephant
17. rhino
18. lion

Hair and There

While on your visit to the zoo today, see how many different things you can find out about the mammals that live in the zoo.

1. Find a mammal:

   with no hair on the face
   without a tail
   that lives in water
   that walks on two feet (look beside you!)

2. Every mammal has a backbone made up of smaller bones called vertebrae. SO DO YOU! Touch the back of your neck with your fingers and feel your vertebrae.

3. Use tally marks to show how many times you can find a mammal with:

   brown hair   white hair
   black hair   red hair
   tan hair   purple hair

   You were unable to find one of these colors of hair. Why? _____

   _____

4.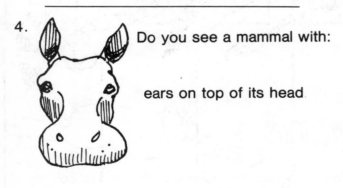

   Do you see a mammal with:

   ears on top of its head

   ears on the side of its head

   Where are your ears?

5. Look at the teeth on these two skulls.

   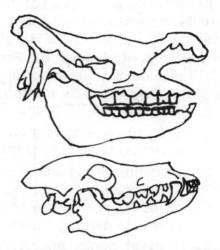

   Which teeth would be good for chewing grass?
   Which teeth would be good for chewing meat?

6. How many toes do you have? Can you find a mammal with the same number of toes? Write the name of that animal below.

   _____

7. Find a mammal with:

   eyes on the front of its head

   eyes on the side of its head

   Why are the eyes in different places?

   _____

   _____

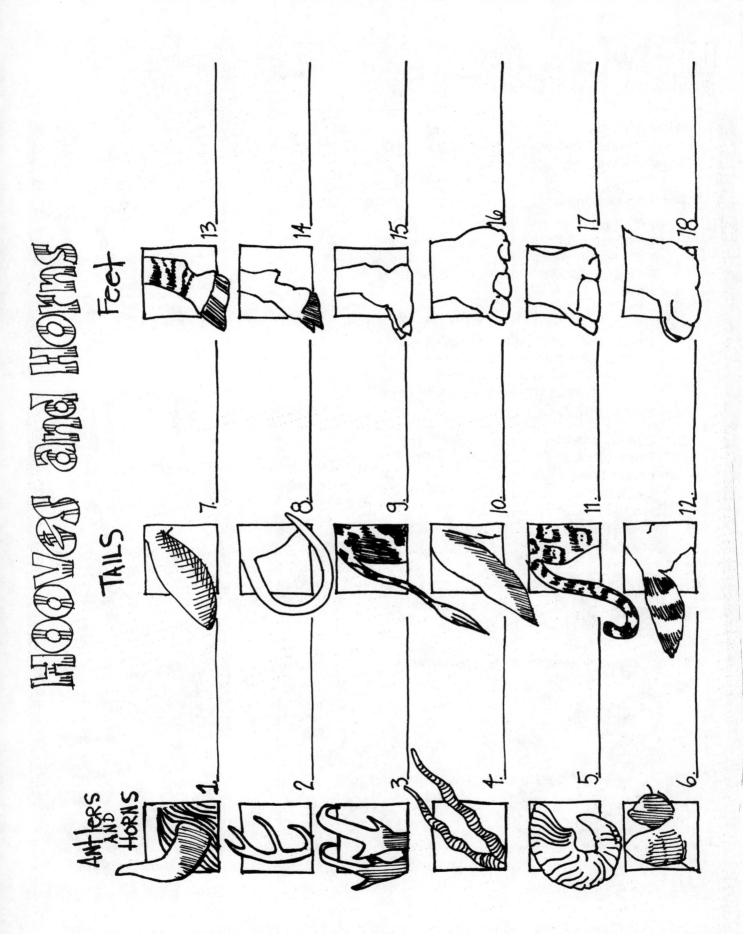

Hooves and Horns

Feet

Antlers
AND
HORNS

TAILS

cheetah

leopard

Jaguar

giraffe

zebra

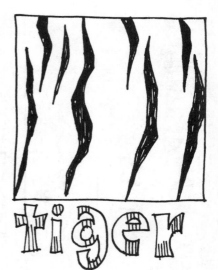

tiger

ocelot

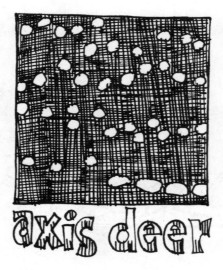

axis deer

okapi

Bird formation

Birds are found everywhere throughout the world. They show a large variety of colors, sizes, shapes and habits. There are 8580 living species of birds which have been assigned by ornithologists to one of twenty-seven major groups or orders.

All birds have one unique and distinguishing characteristic--feathers, which act as an aid for temperature regulation as well as an instrument of flight. When fluffed, feathers hold an insulating layer of warm air which protects the thin, delicate skin. But heat is allowed to escape when the feathers are compressed against the body. The down feathers are the most important type of feather used for insulation.

There are several kinds of feathers on a bird's body. The tail feathers and the long flight feathers of the wings are important in flight and have stiff shafts for strength. The contour feathers cover the body. They are smaller than the flight and tail feathers and do not have a stiff shaft. Underneath the contour feathers are the down feathers.

All birds have feathers; however, some flightless birds have greatly reduced wings and feathers that are too coarse to support the bird in flight. Among those birds that cannot fly are the ostrich, the penguin and the rhea. The bill of a bird is adapted to its way of life, especially its diet. Birds eat every day and often spend much of the day in search of food. The beak of a bird has no teeth. The feet of a bird are also adapted to the bird's way of life. Flightless birds have long toes for running, and birds of prey have strong hooked claws for grasping flesh.

Vision and hearing are the most developed senses in birds. All birds have ear openings in the sides of their heads. Some birds, such as owls, rely more on hearing than vision when they hunt for food. Many birds have a higher density of vision cells in the eye than mammals. No other living thing can match the visual acuity of birds.

Eggs come in many shapes, colors and sizes. The shape and color of the egg is related to the size of the bird. The incubation period of the egg depends on the species. Incubation can be performed by the female only (example: ostrich), the male only (example: emu), or both sexes (example: ostrich).

Birds evolved from reptiles about 130 million years ago but today still possess reptilian characteristics, such as shelled egg, scales on the legs, and an *egg tooth* used by young birds to break open the shell when hatching.

vocabulary

avian:	On the wing; of or related to birds.
aviary:	Large cage that birds live in.
bill:	Jaws of a bird made of bone with an outside covering of a horn-like material (similar to our fingernails).
flock:	Social group in which birds live.
incubation:	Time after eggs are laid before they hatch.
migration:	Seasonal movement of animals between breeding and wintering grounds.
molt:	Loss of old feathers which are replaced by new ones.
ornithology:	The study of birds.
ornithologist:	Person who studies birds.

books for children

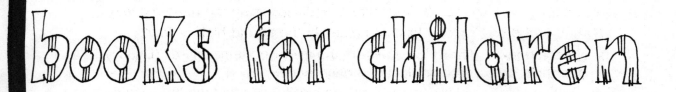

Arnold, Caroline, *Five Nests,* E.P. Dutton.

Brenner, Barbara, *Have You Ever Heard of a Kangaroo Bird?* Thomas Y. Crowell Co.

Cooper, Kay, *C'mon Ducks!* Julian Messner Publishing.

Flanagan, Geraldine and Morris, Sean, *Window into a Nest,* Houghton-Mifflin.

Freedman, Russell, *How Birds Fly,* Holiday House.

Freschet, Bernice, *The Owl and the Prairie Dog,* Charles Scribner's Son.

Gans, Roma, *Birds Eat and Eat and Eat,* Thomas Y. Crowell Co.

Garelick, May, *What Makes a Bird a Bird?* Follett Publishing.

Kaufmann, John, *Birds are Flying,* Thomas Y. Crowell Co.

Prescott, Ernest, *What Comes Out of an Egg?* Franklin Watts.

Schloat, G. Warren, Jr., *The Wonderful Egg,* Scribner & Sons.

Selsam, Milicent, *A First Look at Birds,* Walker and Co.

Selsam, Millicent, *Tony's Birds,* Harper and Row.

Simon, Seymour, *Birds on Your Street,* Holiday House.

Bird Watchers

Although most bird watching enthusiasts will tramp miles through bushes and undergrowth to spot a rare species and observe its reactions, you can learn much about bird behavior by going to the zoo. Find a comfortable spot to sit while watching the antics of your feathered friends. The following birds can be found in most zoos: house sparrow, chicken, pigeon and peacock. Sit quietly and watch for some of the following things:

1. Is the bird found in a group or alone?
2. Does it walk or hop? (If your bird is walking, does the head move?)
3. Is the bird making any kind of noise? Is the sound high or low?
4. Can you see a difference between the male and female bird? (Usually the male is more colorful with showy feathers.)
5. Can you find a color or design on the bird's body that would help you to recognize it?
6. What do the feet and beak look like? How does the bird use them when eating?
7. If your bird flies, can you hear the "takeoff"?
8. Are there any young birds around?

After observing one kind of bird for awhile, begin observing a different species. Compare their behavior. How are they alike or different?

Bird watching is a fun hobby for many people. A list of all the birds spotted by your family or class can be kept. Be careful! Bird watching can become a habit. If you would like to continue bird watching, you can get more information from the National Audubon Society. The address is located in the Racy Resources chapter.

Up, up and away

Since the beginning of time, man has wanted to fly like a bird. We have soared in gliders, floated up in balloons and zoomed through the air in jet planes, but we have never truly "flapped" our own wings. Birds are able to fly because of body adaptations such as hollow bones, reduced size and weight and feathers that catch the air as they fly.

The following experiences will serve as an introduction to flight:

1. Compare the body shapes of a bird and an airplane. How are they alike? How are they different? Now compare specific birds to specific planes. For example:

    hummingbird - helicopter
    duck - seaplane
    falcon - jet

2. To better understand how air pushes against a surface such as a wing, try the following experiment. Take two pieces of paper the same size. Crumple one of them into a ball and leave the other flat. Drop both of them from the same height. The crumpled piece should fall faster.
   Explanation: Both pieces of paper must push through the air to reach the ground. The flat piece of paper has more of its surface exposed to the air. Since there is more air putting pressure on the flat piece of paper, it falls more slowly. How does the surface of a flat piece of paper compare to the surface of a wing?

3. Play some music that might suggest flight and let your younger children try their "wings" at flying, flapping, gliding, soaring, hovering and diving. How do these flying styles differ from each other?

4. Bubbles, homemade parachutes, kites and paper airplanes will provide your students with plenty of chances to interact with air pressure, floating and gravity.

44

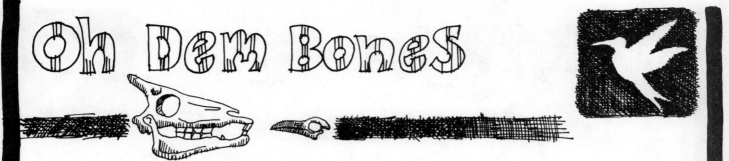

Oh Dem Bones

Birds are adapted for flight in many ways. Their bones are light and hollow which helps to lessen body weight. The skeleton of a three to four-pound frigate bird may weigh as little as four ounces less than the weight of the bird's feathers.

Explore this adaptation for flight with the following activity: Contact a butcher shop or meat packing plant and ask them to save a variety of large mammal and bird bones (lamb, chicken, turkey, beef, pork or rabbit). Clean the bones by boiling them, scraping off the meat and drying them in the sun.

Use the clean bones for weight comparison. Choose sections of mammal and bird bones which are similar in length and circumference. Weigh each bone on a small scale. Older children can graph or chart the weights. Bird bones will weigh less.

Saw the bones down the middle to help children discover the hollow structure of the bird bones. Is this why the bird bones weigh less?

Fancy Feathers

Hoopoe

Birds are one of the groups of animals that have color vision. They use color to assist them in attracting a mate and as camouflage when hiding from a predator.

Use the Fancy Feathers work sheet found at the back of this chapter for some color exploration while you are visiting the zoo.

Before arriving at the zoo, fill in the color boxes with crayons or felt tip pens. The work sheet can then be used to see how many different colors of feathers can be found as well as the location of the feathers and the names of the birds.

Pinch, Peck, and Pull

With most birds the beak is designed for a specific job. Many birds use their beaks as a tool - a hammer or chisel, tweezers, nutcracker or spear. This concept concerning beak adaptation can be introduced with the following activities:

1. Collect a variety of small tools that can be used for comparison to a bird's beak. (See list below.) If possible, find pictures of birds that you are discussing, or use the pictures of both birds and their tools. Use a group discussion time to introduce the tools and explain how certain birds use their beaks as tools. After this introduction, allow children use of the pictures and tools to do further research and discover some new tools.

2. Before your visit to the zoo, find out which birds you will be able to observe. Take along the tools that match those birds in your "zoo bag." Show children which tools you have brought along and have them help to discover the birds that use their beaks like those tools.

BIRD	TOOL	USE
Parrot, cockatoo	Nutcracker	Crack seeds or nuts
Heron, darter	Spear	Impale fish
Woodpecker	Chisel, hammer	Drive into bark to reach insects
Flamingo, duck	Strainer	Filter out mud and water and retain minute plants and animals
Robin	Tweezer	Pinch or pick up food
Pelican	Large net or basket	Trap fish
Puffin	Vise	Crush clams
Hawk, owl, eagle	Meat hook	Tear at meat
Hummingbird	Straw	Obtain nectar

happy hatching

BIRD

AMPHIBIAN

PLATYPUS - AN UNUSUAL egg-LAYING MAMMAL

FISH

Reptile

Discuss the idea that animals other than birds hatch from eggs. Collect at least one large plastic egg for each child. Draw or cut out pictures of different animals that hatch from eggs and place one picture inside each egg. Hide the eggs and let the children find them and discover the animals inside.

Older children can do some home research and bring in pictures of animals that hatch from eggs. These pictures can be used for a large bulletin board display or in playing an egg hunt. The Happy Hatching work sheet can also be used with this activity.

Guawk Parrot Power

Parrots and many other birds of the tropical forests have very brightly colored feathers and loud calls. This combination of bright feathers and loud calls serves as a means of communication which is often needed in the dense foliage of tropical forests.

Have your group imagine that they are living in a dark forest. They can then divide into pairs and make up a call that could be used as a way of communicating - something loud and wild but also easy to recognize as coming from the other partner. Blindfold each child and scatter everyone into an open area. At a signal from the leader, have each pair make their call in an attempt to locate each other. When partners are located, remove the blindfolds and report to the leader. The Parrot Power work sheet can also be used with this activity.

IT'S BALZAC - CALLing COLLEct AGAIN.

A LIVING GREEN NEST

This soft grassy-looking nest is actually thickly sown wheat, bird, or grass seed growing on top of several inches of moistened vermiculite. Be certain to have the children help with this project. Perhaps each child can have his/her very own container (nest) if enough are available.

Containers:

1. Hollowed-out potatoes.
2. Cottage cheese cartons covered with straw, hay or grass. Weave twigs and string into the straw.
3. Straw or wicker baskets lined with plastic wrap to prevent water from draining.
4. Ceramic or clay pots.

Procedure:

Purchase seed and vermiculite from a nursery or a health food store. Line the containers if necessary. Pour in vermiculite, stopping about two inches from the top (one inch if you are using bird seed). Sprinkle a thick layer of seed over the vermiculite. Pour in water until it is just visible beneath the seeds. Porous containers may drip, even with the plastic lining. If this happens, let the water drain off into the sink, set it on a saucer and move to a spot with good light (not directly in the sun).

Lightly cover the top of the container with plastic wrap for two days to hold the moisture before removing it. The seal should not be too tight. There should be enough air to help prevent mold. In three to five days the seeds will begin to sprout. This is a good time to put in the eggs, the rocks and let the "grass" grow around them. In approximately ten days the grass will be almost fully grown. After about fourteen days you will have to throw the grass away.

NEST SCULPTURE

Help children to examine a real bird's nest. Talk about the materials used and how birds secure the materials together to form the nest. Follow this group discussion with a walking trip to collect nest materials. Supplement your findings with extra string and twigs. Children can create their own nests, using glue mixed with water to help hold the materials together.

Birds are the only creatures in the world with feathers! During your next visit to the zoo, conduct a feather search. When your children have a handful of feathers, try the following investigations:

1. Take a close look at the structure of the feather. What is its shape? Draw the feather as you observe it. This will help to focus on the details. Notice the strong shaft running the length of the feather. Is it directly in the center or is it off to one side?

2. Examine the feather with a magnifying glass. The individual parts of the feather (barbs) are hooked together like a zipper. When a bird preens, he pulls on each part of the feather to make certain it is "zipped up." Any open spots along the feather would allow the air to rush through and make flight impossible. Encourage your students to separate the barbs and zip them back together.

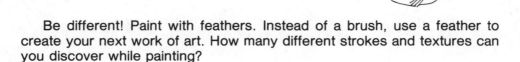

Be different! Paint with feathers. Instead of a brush, use a feather to create your next work of art. How many different strokes and textures can you discover while painting?

After collecting a wide variety of colored feathers, have your children create a feather mobile. To do this, you will need modeling clay, scissors and yarn. Roll a piece of clay into a round ball about the size of a tennis ball. Tie the yarn around the middle and leave a loose end with which to hang the mobile. Stick feathers into the ball until the entire surface is covered. You may also add dry flowers to the arrangement. Hang the finished creation and enjoy.

Edible Nest

8 large shredded wheat biscuits (crumbled)
1 12-oz. jar peanut butter
1 12-oz. package butterscotch chips

Mix peanut butter and butterscotch chips together and melt over low heat. Gradually add crumbled shredded wheat until the mixture is thick in consistency. The mixture should have a "grassy" look (add water if it seems too thick).

Give each child a piece of wax paper with his name on it. Place one large spoonful of the mixture on each square of wax paper and cool slightly. Allow each child to shape his own nest. Harden in the refrigerator for fifteen to twenty minutes and fill with raisins or nuts for a really fun snack! This recipe makes approximately fifteen nests.

Hats, Hats, Hats

Take advantage of the spring season to make some original millinery creations. Encourage children to use their imaginations in using birds as their theme. The base can be any shape (cone, sphere, box, etc.) so long as it fits on the head of its creator. Hats can become large eggs with a chick peeking out or a tree with a nest and bird among its branches. Hands can be traced, colored and transformed into wonderful chickens or turkeys. Think big and make a hat for two people to wear. SHAZAM! The world's largest walking bird nest.

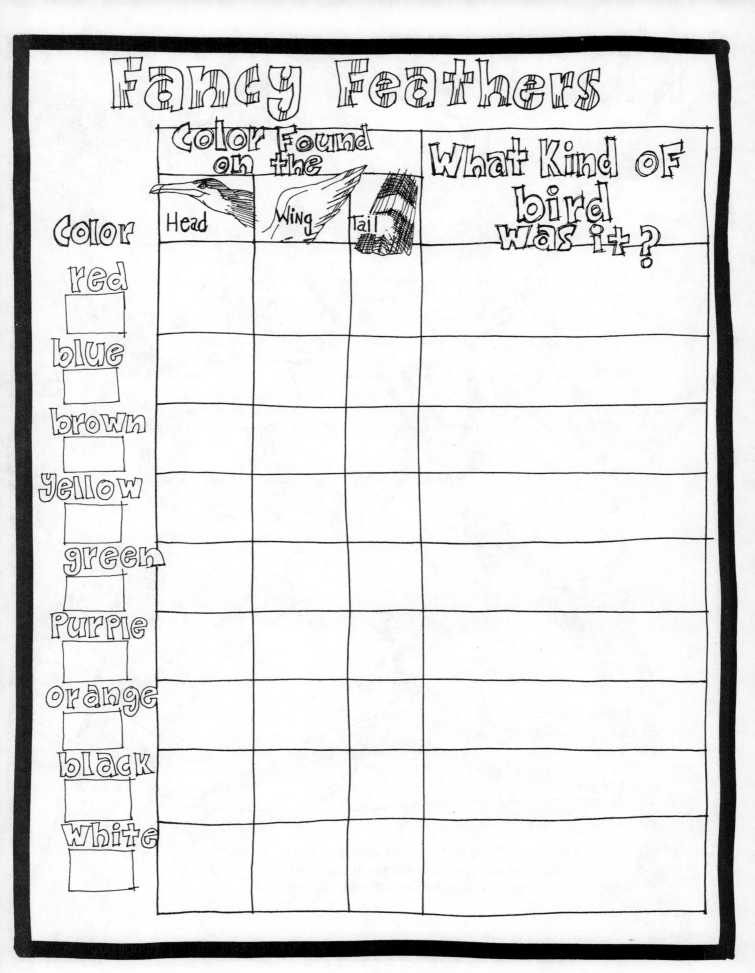

Fancy Feathers

Color	Color Found on the Head	Wing	Tail	What Kind OF bird was it?
red				
blue				
brown				
Yellow				
green				
Purple				
orange				
black				
White				

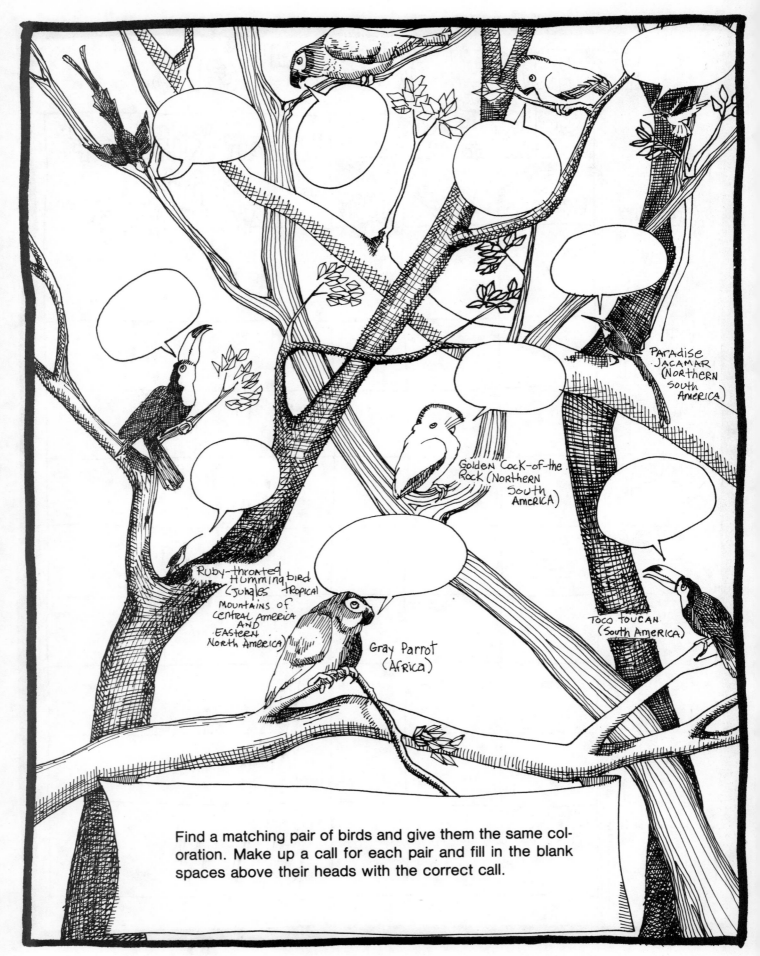

Find a matching pair of birds and give them the same coloration. Make up a call for each pair and fill in the blank spaces above their heads with the correct call.

Reptileformation

The reptiles are a very old class of vertebrates. For 100 million years, the dinosaurs ruled the earth and then they mysteriously disappeared.

Only five kinds of reptiles have survived to the present day: the crocodilians, the turtles, the lizards and snakes, and the lizard-like tuatara.

All reptiles have scales. The scales are tough and are made of a nonliving tissue. Like the hair of mammals and the feathers of birds, the scales are made up of dead horny tissues containing the protein *keratin.* In crocodilians, turtles and snakes the large scales are called *scutes.*

All reptiles shed their skin periodically. The number of times they shed depends upon the diet, the age and general health of the animal. Snakes shed their skin in one long piece, crawling out of the old skin and turning it inside out as they crawl out. Most lizards shed their skin in patches while crocodilians and turtles shed one plate at a time. Young reptiles shed more often than older ones because they are growing.

Most reptiles have teeth which are also shed and replaced frequently. Some snakes, especially the poisonous ones, have special teeth called fangs. These fangs are hollow and are used to inject venom into prey. Turtles do not have teeth but have a sharp horny beak which is sometimes serrated.

Reptiles have no effective mechanism for the regulation of body heat. Their temperature rises and falls according to the temperature of the surrounding air or water. This is why reptiles are called *cold-blooded.* They are more tolerant of low temperatures. They have no sweat glands, so their only effective means of avoiding heat is to seek shade. The main method of raising their body temperature is basking in the sun.

Some reptiles lay eggs and some experience live birth. A few reptiles build nests for their eggs. The young are on their own at birth or hatching, and they are fully equipped to face the world.

Reptiles have a poorly developed sense of sight and hearing. The sense of touch is fairly acute, especially in snakes which are able to detect other approaching animals from vibrations received through the ground. Snakes are deaf and lack external ear openings.

Snakes and lizards have a special sense organ located in the roof of the mouth called *Jacobson's organ.* This is a cavity in the palate of the reptile where a large number of nerves are connected to the brain. The forked tongue is inserted into Jacobson's organ where particles of smell and taste are analyzed. This is the reason that snakes and lizards are frequently seen "tasting" or "smelling" the air by flicking the tongue in and out.

Reptiles are one group of animals that many people tend to fear. Most of these fears are due to a lack of information or misunderstanding. Generally, they are peaceable, secretive animals that try to avoid confrontations with other species, including man. As a group, reptiles benefit mankind in many ways and should be treated with respect and should be recognized as the marvelous creatures which they are.

ooooos and aaaahs

Many people are fascinated with interesting facts about reptiles. Here are a few amazing reptile statistics to dazzle your students.

1. Largest reptile - saltwater crocodile
2. Fastest reptile - six-lined racer (18 miles per hour)
3. Largest lizard - komodo dragon (365 lbs, 8' 4'')
4. Longest snake - reticulate python from Southeast Asia (33 feet in length)
5. African egg-eating snake - can swallow eggs twice its width. It has sharp bones in the neck area which break the shell. The egg is swallowed and the shell is spit out.
6. Sea snake - can swim 1000 miles out to sea.
7. Spitting cobra - can spit poison into the eyes of another animal.

Vocabulary

antivenin:	Serum used to fight against a reptile's venom when a person or animal is bitten by a poisonous snake.
aquatic:	Live in the water or spend most of the time there.
carapace:	Top of a turtle or tortoise shell.
constrictor:	A snake that kills prey by squeezing it with its coils.
fangs:	Modified hollow teeth that are used to inject venom.
herbivore:	An animal that eats only plant material - example: California desert tortoise.
herpetologist:	A person that studies reptiles and amphibians.
Jacobson's organ:	A thin membrane of skin that tells a reptile what is around him by translating small chemical particles brought in from the air. This organ is located in the roof of the mouth.
plastron:	The bottom of a turtle or tortoise shell.
predator:	An animal that eats other animals.
scutes:	Enlarges scales (some are located on the underneath side of a snake.)
venom:	A poisonous secretion that destroys the proper function of liquids or nerve endings in an animal's body.

books for children

Anderson, Lonzo and Adams Adrienne, *Izzard,* Scribners & Sons.

Blassingame, Wyatt, *The Wonders of the Turtle,* Dodd Mead & Co.

Carrick, Carol, *The Crocodiles Still Wait,* Houghton Mifflin.

Conklin, Gladys, and Marokvia, Artur, *I Caught a Lizard,* Holiday House.

Daly, Kathleen, *Dinosaurs,* Golden Press.

Daly, Kathleen, *A Child's Book of Snakes, Lizards, and Other Reptiles,* Doubleday.

Freshet, Bernice, *Lizard Lying in the Sun,* Charles Scribner's & Sons.

Gross, Ruth Belov, *Alligators and Other Crocodilians,* Four Winds Press.

Hoff, Syn, *Danny and the Dinosaur,* Random House.

May, Julian, *The Warm-Blooded Dinosaurs,* Holiday House.

McGowen, Ton, *Album of Reptiles,* Rand McNally.

Peterson, Esther Allen, *Frederick's Alligator,* Crown Publishers.

Rowe, Erna, *Giant Dinosaurs,* Scholastic-TAB-Publications.

Selsam, Millicent E., *Let's Get Turtles,* Harper & Row.

Simon, Seymour, *Discovering What Garter Snakes Do,* McGraw - Hill.

Waber, Bernard, *Lyle, Lyle, Crocodile,* Houghton Mifflin.

Captive Care

If you are looking for a classroom animal, you might consider keeping a reptile. Reptiles make excellent pets. They don't have to be brushed; they can survive over a weekend without food and they don't smell.

A basic cage would consist of a ten-gallon terrarium with a heat source of some kind. Most tropical fish stores will sell their "leaker" aquariums at a reduced rate.

There are specific requirements for keeping each type of reptile in captivity.

SNAKES

Snakes are notorious escape artists. Be certain that the lid on your terrarium is trapped and weighted down. Most snakes should be housed at a temperature between 75 and 80 degrees. Pine shavings or newspapers can be used to line the cage bottom. A hiding place can be made from an empty milk carton. Cut a hole in the side large enough for your snake to crawl inside. You should provide fresh drinking water at all times. Your snake can be fed once weekly. The type of food will depend upon the snake. King snakes will eat mice, gopher snakes eat mice and small birds and larger boas and pythons eat rats and rabbits. DO NOT LEAVE LIVE RODENTS IN WITH YOUR SNAKE. THEY CAN CRIPPLE OR KILL YOUR PET.

LIZARDS

Lizards can be a problem in captivity. Many of them need high temperatures and special lighting as well as a diet of live insects or fresh plant material depending upon the species of lizard. Avoid a steady diet of mealworms. Be certain to provide a climbing area near the heat source so that the lizard can bask in the heat. It is natural for lizards to experience a body temperature drop at night, so the heat source can be turned off each day when you leave the classroom. If your lizard seems shy, provide it with a hiding place. Fresh water at all times is also a necessity.

WATER TURTLES

As the name implies, turtles will need a body of water in which they can swim. An aquarium partially filled with water is ideal. Most turtles need a place to climb out of the water so they don't drown. A high protein goldfish pellet or trout chow is best for a balanced daily diet. Fresh, raw liver of beef can also be provided on a periodic basis. Avoid commercial turtle food. It is made up of dried insect skeletons and is nutritionally deficient. It is important to know that many water turtles can't feed unless their heads are submerged underwater.

TORTOISES

If you are keeping a tortoise inside a terrarium, do not cover the cage bottom with sand or gravel. It will stick to the food when the tortoise eats. The animal can become impacted and die. The best substrate is a commercial cat litter that is made up of 100 percent alfalfa pellets. Tortoises are vegetarians. Fresh fruits and vegetables should be sprinkled with a powdered vitamin supplement once each week. Fresh water should be available, but bear in mind that tortoises can drown. They are not adapted for swimming. Your tortoise should be allowed to graze on the lawn and sun itself occasionally.

For further information, contact your zoo herpetologist or university zoology department. Pet shops rarely have correct information on captive reptile care.

Dinosaur Fun

There is a current controversy over dinosaurs. Some scientists believe they were cold-blooded reptiles, others believe they were warm-blooded bird-like creatures. Warm or cold they were some of the largest vertebrates that have ever lived on Earth.

In order for your students to understand how big these creatures were, have them do the following:

Split the class in teams of 3 or 4. Give each team a tape measure. Let each team select a dinosaur from the dinosaur chart found in the back of this chapter. Select a grassy area and have each team measure off the size of their dinosaur. Mark the measured length with pieces of yarn or similar material. Compare the sizes.

Ask the following questions:

1. How many children can fit inside a brontosaurus? (After marking off the length of the chosen dinosaur, lay the children down head to toe along the measured length and find out the answer.)

2. Since dinosaurs were so large, what would they have had to eat in order to survive?

3. Where would dinosaurs live if they were alive today?

4. If the zoo had a dinosaur what type of exhibit would it need?

Reptile Rumors

The following game can be used to help children identify factual statements about reptiles. It can also be adapted for nonreaders who can learn to identify pictures of reptiles.

The gameboard consists of two 9" x 12" tagboard pieces which are taped together so that they can stand up in front of the student. Each tagboard piece should have a pocket on it to hold 3" x 5" cards. Label one side "rumor" and the other "truth" (or reptile and nonreptile). You can also use humorous drawings to symbolize rumor or truth.

Make up 3" x 5" cards with statements about reptiles (or select pictures of reptiles and other animals). Make each card self-checking by listing the correct answer on the back or by using the correct symbol. Listed below are some statements that might be included on your cards.

1. A snake can use its tongue as a stinger.(Rumor-A snake uses its tongue as an important sense organ.)
2. The brontosaurus was a reptile that ate plants. (Truth)
3. There is only one kind of tuatara. (Truth)
4. The largest reptiles on Earth are the boa constrictors. (Rumor-The largest reptiles are the crocodilians.)
5. Tortoises and turtles have sharp teeth for eating. (Rumor-They bite food with their bony beak-like jaws.)
6. Snakes shed their skins only once each year. (Rumor-They shed frequently as they grow larger.)
7. Snakes keep growing until they die. (Truth)
8. All snakes are slimy. (Rumor-The skin of a snake is clean and soft.)
9. Some snakes can milk cows. (Rumor-Snakes have no sucking ability.)
10. You can tell the age of a rattlesnake by the number of its rattles. (Rumor-It gets a new rattle every time it sheds its skin, which is more than once each year.

Meringue Monsters

Young cooks can learn the basics of using a pastry bag and at the same time can create their favorite snake, dinosaur or reptile "monsters." A pastry bag fitted with a tip that has a closed star pattern or a large decorator tip is the easiest for little hands to maneuver. Egg whites should be at room temperature and all bowls, spoons and beaters should be grease-free. Line your *greased* cookie sheets with brown paper and try not to squeeze the "monsters" too thinly onto the paper. Short, thick shapes are less likely to break.

The recipe:

4 egg whites (about ½ cup)
1 cup sugar
½ teaspoon lemon juice
½ teaspoon vanilla

Use an electric mixer to beat the egg whites until foamy. Add lemon juice and beat until soft peaks begin to form. Add sugar, one tablespoon at a time, beating constantly at high speed. The mixture should form stiff glossy peaks. Beat in vanilla.

Spoon meringue into pastry bags, squeeze slowly onto paper-lined baking sheets. Decorate with raisins for eyes and sliced almonds for scales. Bake at 200° for one to one and one-half hours until dry. Remove with a spatula to a flat surface to cool. Store in airtight containers. This recipe makes approximately twenty-five three-inch cookies.

MERINGUE MAGIC MAKES MAGNIFICENT MONSTERS!!

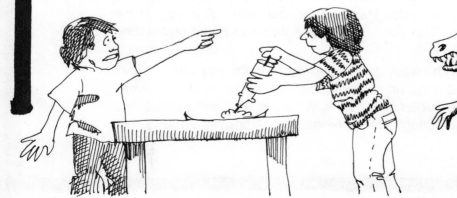

Reptile Parade

Stir those creative juices one more time by helping your students to design their own special "Huge Herps." Children should be divided into teams since their creations will require more than one person to handle. The head of each reptile can start with any shape cardboard box that is large enough to cover the top portion of a child. Team members can choose one from among them to serve as the head. Cut out a large mouth and eyes and decorate with paint, paper and construction paper.

The rest of the reptile is made from a long piece of butcher paper which has been covered with scales and legs. One child directs the head while the other team members climb under the body and help to move their reptile along. Have all teams line up their "Huge Herps" for a reptile parade around the school.

Rub -a- Reptile

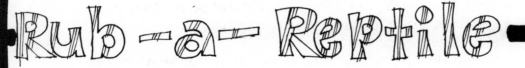

Contact your local pet store owner or zoo herpetologist and ask him to collect snake sheddings for you. Perhaps he can also give you some scales from a tortoise or turtle shell. Use these items to make interesting nature rubbings.

Provide each child with paper and crayons, pencils and chalk. Have children place their sheddings or scales under the paper and rub gently with their crayons. Each rubbing will look different and will appear like magic before their eyes. Collect the rubbings and arrange them together as a large wall mural.

Leapin' Lizards

Leapin' Lizards is a fun game that will help your students to identify some of the common reptiles. For each playing card, make a copy of the Leapin' Lizards work sheet found in the back of this chapter. Cut the squares apart and arrange the pictures in a different sequence for each card. Glue them to a piece of cardboard and cover the board with clear Con-Tact paper. Provide each player with several markers. Buttons, bottle caps or paper "scales" will also work.

Below are two versions of the game. You can also create your own if you like.

VERSION ONE:

Place the names of the different reptiles in a bowl. One person draws a name and calls it out loud to the other players. As a name is called, players cover the animal's picture with a marker. The first person who covers five pictures in a row is the winner of the game.

VERSION TWO:

The simple statements listed below are placed in a bowl. One of the players draws a clue and reads it out loud. Other players must then guess which reptile fits the statement and cover that reptile's picture.

alligator: A large aquatic reptile that lives in swamps.

boa constrictor: A large snake famous for squeezing its prey.

chameleon: A long tongue and turret-like eyes make this color-changing lizard unique.

cobra: A poisonous snake with a hood.

coral snake: A red-white-and-black poisonous snake.

crocodile: A heavily scaled aquatic reptile with a long snout.

desert tortoise: A land tortoise that lives in the dry deserts of California and Nevada. California state reptile.

Galapagos tortoise: A giant tortoise.

garter snake: A frog and fish-eating snake.

gecko: These small lizards can hold on to the side of a wall with their specialized toes.

gavial: A rare crocodile with long thin jaws from India.

Gila monster: A poisonous lizard native to the United States.

gopher snake: A common rodent-eating snake.

green iguana: A large plant-eating lizard from Central and South America.

king snake: A harmless snake to man that is a cannibal.

komodo dragon: The world's largest lizard.

matamata turtle: A turtle with a long nose and neck. It is camouflaged to look like dead leaves.

monitor: A dragon-like lizard with a forked tongue.

racer: A long fast snake that is active during warm weather.

rattlesnake: A snake that is poisonous and makes noise with its tail.

red-eared turtle: A common water turtle with red on its neck.

reticulate python: The longest snake in the world.

rhinoceros viper: A poisonous snake with "horns" on its nose.

sea turtle: This ocean-dwelling turtle has large flattened flippers to help it swim.

snapping turtle: A meat-eating water turtle with powerful jaws.

Rainbow Reptiles

Tape together several sheets of butcher paper. Draw and cut out the outline of any reptile (turtle, snake, alligator, lizard). Randomly cut the animal into different shapes and number the back of each. Remember the sequence as you will have to put them back together again in the proper order.

Provide paint, construction paper, glue, tissue paper, crayons, felt tip pens and assorted collage materials. Pass out a shape to each child and let him decorate the shape in wild colors and designs. Collect the completed shapes and tape them back into their original sequence. Hang them on the wall and surprise your students with their very own Rainbow Reptiles.

Masked Marvels

Reptiles have evolved over millions of years to exist in their present form. Every horn, frill and color or pattern has been developed as a result of the animal adapting to its environment. By creating their own masks, children can focus on the unique facial features of reptiles. They can also sharpen their observation skills and learn to identify the characteristics of different reptiles.

A simple mask shape can be made by folding a sheet of paper in three places to form a cube. Scales can be fashioned out of sequins, buttons, shiny cellophane or colored paper. As your students begin constructing their masks, be certain they notice the following: the size and number of horns, the shape and pattern of scales, the placement of the eyes (whether they are in front or on the side of the head), and if there are any colors or destinctive markings on the head. Ask children to share their creations with the rest of the group.

Fearsome Foes?

Reptiles are one group of animals that people tend to fear. A general lack of knowledge or a misrepresentation of facts can develop these fears at an early age. Young children tend to model behavior exhibited by the adults surrounding them. An adult's fear can easily be passed on to a child.

When studying reptiles, the following ideas should be reinforced:

    a. There are *no* bad or mean animals. It is wrong to assign human emotions to animals. We simply do not know if they feel as we do.

    b. Each animal has an important role to play in the environment.

    c. Animals do not aggressively attack people. They will defend themselves if hurt or frightened.

Play acting is an acceptable way for children to release their fears while they learn more about these misunderstood creatures. Divide the class into four teams. Give each group a card with one of the following situations written on it:

1. Present a commercial entitled "The Snake Speaks," where the snake gives its opinions on how people treat his fellow reptiles.

2. Some kids are camping with their parents. A snake comes into camp and everyone must decide whether to kill it or not.

3. Your class is on a trip to the zoo and one of your friends is afraid of reptiles. What would you do to help him not to be afraid?

4. Your brother has a snake and tries to scare two of your friends by holding the snake in their faces. What would you do?

Each group must decide how they will present their situation to the rest of the class. Several different methods of dramatization can be used. Children can hold a debate, conduct a panel discussion, present a pantomime without using words, or construct junk puppets and perform a show for the rest of the class.

OH BOTHER!

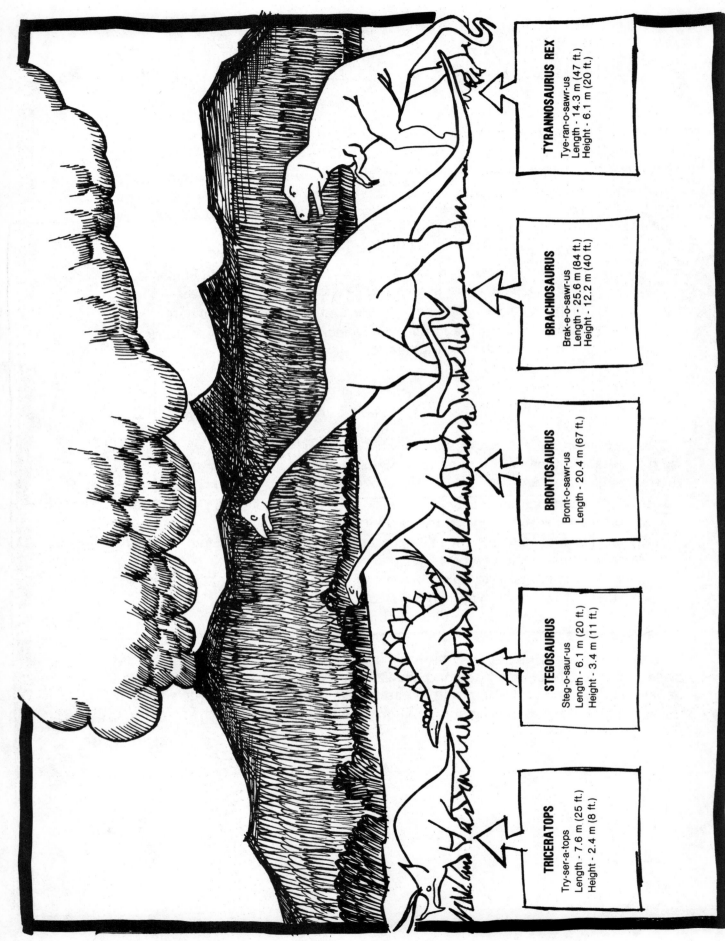

TYRANNOSAURUS REX

Tye-ran-o-sawr-us
Length - 14.3 m (47 ft.)
Height - 6.1 m (20 ft.)

BRACHIOSAURUS

Brak-e-o-sawr-us
Length - 25.6 m (84 ft.)
Height - 12.2 m (40 ft.)

BRONTOSAURUS

Bront-o-sawr-us
Length - 20.4 m (67 ft.)

STEGOSAURUS

Steg-o-sawr-us
Length - 6.1 m (20 ft.)
Height - 3.4 m (11 ft.)

TRICERATOPS

Try-ser-a-tops
Length - 7.6 m (25 ft.)
Height - 2.4 m (8 ft.)

Leapin' Lizards

gopher snake
king cobra
gavial
Galapagos tortoise
chameleon

diamondback rattlesnake
vine snake
alligator snapping turtle
matamata turtle
leaf-tailed gecko

rhinocerous viper
western racer
redear slider
soft shell turtle
Komodo dragon

western coral snake
garter snake
gopher tortoise
sea iguana
Nile monitor

boa constrictor
California king snake
leatherback turtle
Gila monster
crocodile

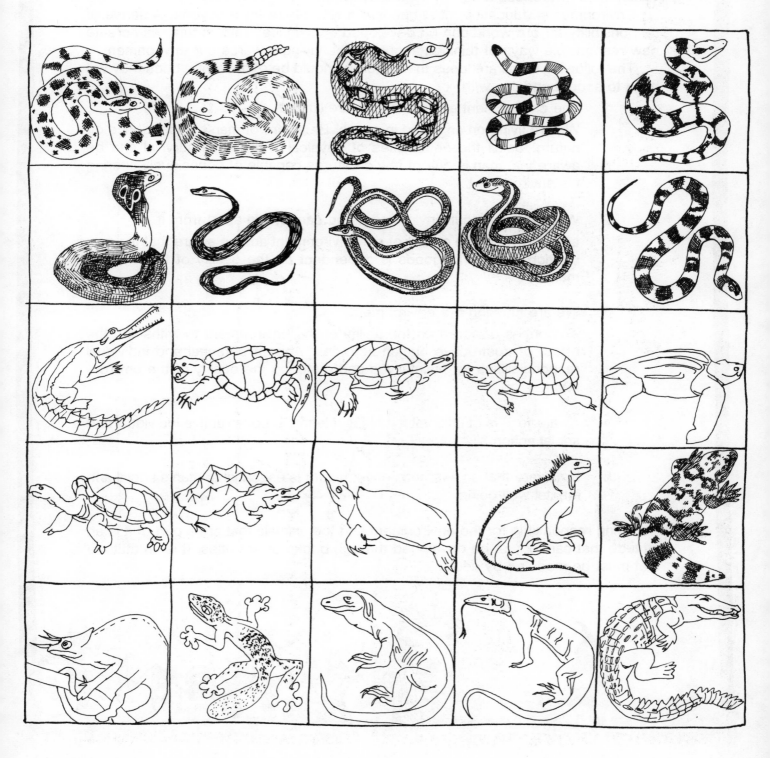

Ecoformation

The environmental movement which began in the 1960's has changed the way most people relate to the land, its resources and to each other. Environmental education began to appear in many classrooms, and family units began to make environmental awareness a part of their daily lives.

Environmental education must become a way of life for everyone. A sense of responsibility for our world can be developed early in life. This, in turn, can create new responsible ways of thinking about and behaving towards our environment.

The following items are ideas that children should be exposed to, ones they will have to accept and live with:

1. The environment and resources are limited.

    We are living on an island in space. Be aware of man's dependence on nature for all the necessities of physical and mental survival and be aware that man is one of few creatures capable of consciously altering his environment.

2. We are part of our environment and cannot live apart from it.

    Learn to value the quality of our environment and be aware that the production of material goods is dependent on the quality of the environment.

3. We are harming our environment.

    Authorities disagree on the ability of the environment to withstand the effect of destructive human activities. Accept personal and individual responsibilities for maintaining and restoring the quality of the environment.

4. Awareness is of little value unless it leads to constructive individual and social action.

5. Be aware that an aesthetic environment is essential to man's social and mental well-being.

Being responsible for the environment and the animals that are a part of it is an attitude that cannot just be developed through books or activities. It is an attitude that must be modeled by adults.

68

Most zoos can provide your children with an environment that exhibits a strong commitment to animal preservation and environmental concern.

Today many zoos are beginning to change their animal environments. They are replacing small, cramped cages with larger enclosures that closely resemble the animal's natural habitat. Animals are allowed to move more freely and as a result are healthier. The new environments have also helped with breeding and caring for the young. People also benefit because they are able to see how the animal might behave in the wild.

Zoos are now also becoming places for study and research. Zoo employees are actively involved in seeking ways to protect wild animals, establishing programs for reproduction, and working on diet and maintenance plans that will help the animals to live longer. For some species the zoo is the only hope for survival.

Some zoos are also active participants in a special computerized program called I.S.I.S., which is designed for census, inventory and vital statistics of animals in captivity. Special emphasis has been placed on species currently on endangered lists. Zoo directors use this system to help with breeding as well as with placement of new animals or replacement of animals that have died. This system is an important step in the zoo's struggle with endangered species.

The government has also passed many laws which have been directed toward the preservation of wildlife. One of the most recent is the Endangered Species Act of 1973. Among its provisions is an authorization to prepare a list of "threatened" species which would also receive federal protection. It also prohibits any federal action that would damage habitat deemed critical to an endangered or threatened species. Fish, reptiles, amphibians, birds and mammals all are represented on the list of endangered species found in the United States and Puerto Rico. This list is subject to periodic revision and a free copy can be obtained by writing the National Wildlife Federation or the Office of Endangered Species. Both addresses can be found in the Racy Resources chapter.

All of these things done by people, zoos and governments should be explained to children. The hope for the future of endangered animals lies in the hands of children who must grow up with a good understanding of what it means to "protect" our environment and its wildlife.

Vocabulary

adaptation: Any change in an animal's structure or function through selection which enables it to survive and reproduce in its environment.

aquatic: Living in water.

biodegradable: Capable of being decomposed by natural biological processes.

conservation: Protection and use of natural resources.

ecology: The study of the interrelationships of animals and plants to the environment.

ecosphere: The natural environment of the planet earth where all known life systems exist.

ecosystems: Separate yet interrelated communities of living things which comprise the ecosphere.

endangered animals: When more animals of a species die than are reproduced.

environment: Natural surroundings of an animal.

extinct: An animal species no longer in existence.

food chain: A concept model which shows how all plants and animals are linked together because each one eats or is eaten by another.

habitat: The natural or usual dwelling place of an individual or group.

natural selection: A process which allows survival of those animals having characteristics that will enable them to adapt to an environment.

poach: To take (game or fish) by illegal methods.

rare: Animals with small populations that are not at present endangered or vulnerable, but are at risk.

terrestrial: Living or growing on land.

threatened: Animal believed likely to move into the endangered category in the near future.

wildlife preserves: Natural places in which wildlife is protected and preserved.

books for children

Adler, Irving, *The Environment,* The John Day Company.
Billington, Elizabeth, *Understanding Ecology,* Warne.
Caputo, Robert, *More Than Just Pets,* Cowerd, McCann and Geoghegen.
Gordon, Esther S. and Gordon, Bernard E., *Once There Was a Passenger Pigeon,* Henry Z. Walck.
Hurd, Edith and Clement, *Wilson's World,* Harper & Row.
Jacobs, Francine, *Sewer Sam: The Sea Cow,* Walker.
Lauber, Patricia, *Too Much Garbage,* Garrard.
Lyth, Mike, *The War on Pollution,* Priory Press.
Moidion, Jon, *Beautiful Junk,* Little Brown.
Miles, Betty, *Save the Earth, an Ecology Handbook for Kids,* Alfred A. Knopf, Inc.
Pringle, Lawrence, *The Only Earth We Have,* Macmillan.
Seuss, Dr. *The Lorax,* Random House.
Simon, Seymour, *Science Projects in Ecology,* Holiday House.
Tresselt, Alvin, *The Dead Tree,* Parents Magazine Press.
Zion, Genee, *Dear Garbage Man,* Harper & Row.

Home Sweet Habitat

Animals live in different places. The specific place an animal lives is known as its habitat. For example, the habitat of a trout is in a cold, running river or stream. The habitat of an elephant is grassland and the forests of Africa.

Use the beanbag game described here as an introduction to animals and habitats. The gameboard can be made out of thin plywood or heavy cardboard. Draw or paint pictures of a tree, a cave, a burrow and a pond. Leave plenty of space between each picture so that you will have room to cut a hole in each picture. Use the simple shapes drawn on this page as a guide for making your own beanbags.

Children can take turns at throwing the beanbag animals at the correct habitat target. An easier version of this game could be created by making it into a flannel board where the child must match the animal to its habitat.

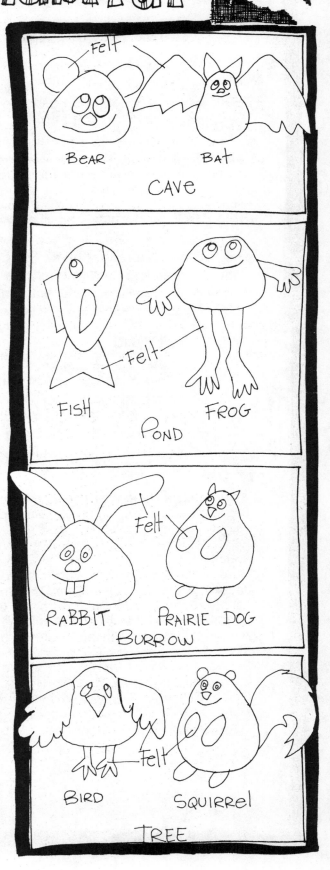

Terrific Trash

TERRIFIC TRASH

The more advanced our society becomes, the more trash we seem to make. Everywhere you look you can see trash that pollutes our rivers and streams, ruins our countryside and litters our streets. The important concept of recycling can be taught by using trash to make new products. Pick up that litter and use what you can to create something that is fun. The best way to make fun out of trash is to turn it into toys or something fun to use. Let the list below spark your creativity and recycle that trash.

EMPTY PAPER TUBES

1. Make a kazoo--wrap a piece of wax paper around one end and secure it with a rubber band. Punch a hole about one inch from the end, pucker and hum through the open end.
2. Finger puppets--decorate with more trash scraps (bottle caps, string, Popsicle sticks, etc.), put over your fingers and have fun.

STRING

STRAW

PAPER Tube

MILK CARTONS

1. Sailboats--cut half-gallon size down one long edge and across the top. Fold open, cut notch in middle to hold paper plate sail. Insert sail and float away.
2. Blocks--cut to desired size, use two blocks inserted together for a better shape. Fill blocks with sand for stability.

PLASTIC or RUBBER PRODUCTS

STRAWS

1. Strawhorn--flatten out one inch of the end, trim the flattened end to a "V." Put cut end of straw into your mouth behind your lips and blow hard.
2. Bubble blower--slice end of straw an an angle. Dip sliced end into bubble solution and blow gently.

PLASTIC BAGS

Parachute--measure a 12-inch square and punch a small hole in each corner. Tie a piece of string through each hole, bring string pieces together and tie through a weight.

PLASTIC SIX-PACK HOLDER

Bubble blower--Dip holder in soapy solution and wave it through the air. Try turning around quickly in circles.

Thumbtack
Clay

PLASTIC BOTTLES

1. Bleach bottle scoops--cut bottles at an angle on the bottom end. Leave handles in place. Use these for sand or tossing a foam or yarn ball.
2. Bottle people--Use bottle shape to determine the personality of your person. Make arms out of cloth or pipe cleaners stuck into the sides of the bottle.

PLASTIC LIDS

Lacing cards--punch holes in lid with a hole punch; use yarn or string to practice lacing or weaving a design.

METAL PRODUCTS

EMPTY CANS

1. Insect cage--use two empty tuna or pineapple ring cans and a length of wire screen six inches wide and long enough to go around inside of cans plus one inch. Shape screen into a tube to fit inside cans, fasten screen together, fit cans over each end of screen.
2. Telephone or walkie-talkie--use two cans of similar size leaving one end open and the other end closed. Make a hole in the center of the closed end, tie cans together with a long piece of string. Stretch the line taut and speak into one can while someone listens.
3. Tin can castle--use your imagination and lots of different-sized cans. Paste on paper windows, doors and towers.

CRUMPLED PAPER

Plastic lid

CARDBOARD

CAN LABELS

Plastic bottle

Begin setting up your own classroom "junk" resource center and invite other classes to use your recyclables for inexpensive projects. Read the book *Beautiful Junk* which is listed in the book list in this chapter. Have your students use materials from your resource center to build their own towers.

Zoo School

Most zoos can provide your group with a special "classroom" for a study on endangered species and the preservation of wildlife. Endangered or threatened animals are usually identified in some way near their enclosure, or you can obtain a list from the zoo office.

Take a special day to visit the endangered or threatened animals only. Use the following questions to help you with a "mini" study on each animal. Adults with younger children can write the answers down as you do a group discussion about each animal.

Here is some important information that should be introduced to children when discussing endangered species.

1. Over the years the number of people in the world has increased. This population increase has caused people to need more space to live in and grow food. Many times animal habitats have been destroyed in order to obtain this needed space.
2. Without their habitats many wild animals cannot survive. Some die because they cannot find enough to eat. Others have no place in which to raise their young or hide from their enemies.
3. Each animal has a special thing to do (its niche) within its habitat. Most animals cannot be moved to another type of habitat because they are not able to adapt to a different niche. The animals that might adapt would then disrupt the environment for the other animals living in that environment.
4. When all the animals of one group die, that species becomes *extinct.* Animals in danger of becoming extinct are called *endangered animals.*

Listed below are some endangered animals and suggestions for study questions. You will have to adapt your questions to the animals your local zoo has.

Polar Bear

Overhunted for Trophies

1. Why would people want to kill this animal?
2. How can we enjoy the animal without killing it?

Asian Elephant

Forest land taken away and changed into farm land.

1. Why would people need more land to farm?
2. Why does taking away its habitat threaten the elephant?

Orangutan

Forest land is being cut for lumber.

1. Why would people want all that lumber?
2. What happens to the orangutan if it doesn't have a forest to live in?
3. What else could be done besides cutting down all the trees for lumber?

Siberian or Bengal Tiger

Overhunted for beautiful fur or as trophies. Habitat being destroyed.

1. Why would people want to kill this animal?
2. What do people use the fur for?
3. What can we do so that people won't kill the tiger for its fur?

Prairie Dog

Poisoned by cattle ranchers until few were left (competition for grass, holes for burrows dangerous).

1. Why would cattle ranchers be upset with the prairie dog?
2. What would have been a better way to slow down the population?

Golden Eagle

Overhunted by sheep ranchers because they thought the eagles were eating their lambs.

1. Was this a problem that could have been prevented? How?
2. What does the golden eagle really eat?
3. Could the eagle help the rancher in any way?

Crocodile

Poaching for hides to use for clothing products. Habitat land taken away.

1. How could we help stop the poaching?
2. What could we do so that people would not make the products out of alligator and crocodile hides?

Predator···Prey

Man has been hunting for survival since the beginning of his existence. Down through the ages hunter and hunted have lived in harmony. That is until man began to develop his modern powered weapons that could decimate an entire species if not carefully controlled.

Today, the issue of hunting is highly emotional one. Explore the issue further with your children by responding to the following questions and activities:

1. Have your kids research the history of big game hunting. What animals were hunted and why? Which were considered to be the most dangerous?
2. What is a "Grand Slam"?
3. What are the current laws and regulations on big game hunting in the United States, Africa and India?
4. Do a biography on some of the most famous hunters--Teddy Roosevelt or Roy Rogers, for example, or write about men or women with an opposing view like Albert Schweitzer.
5. What animals have become extinct from overhunting?
6. Discuss hunting. Is it morally right? Separate the class according to their opinions on this issue and hold a debate.
7. Invite speakers to your class from 300, the S.P.C.A., Sportsman's Club, Ducks Unlimited, or the Audubon Society. Find out how these groups feel about hunting.
8. What are some alternatives to hunting wildlife in our modern society?
9. How do your students feel about hunting? Find out what laws have been passed to protect animals from overhunting.
10. Compare primitive hunting tools like snares, bows and arrows, and spears to modern hunting techniques such as the use of long-distance rifles with scopes, the use of helicopters to hunt from and automatic harpoons.

Each animal occupies a special niche within the environment. Niche has been defined as an animal's special function within its habitat. In other words, niche is what the animal does for "it's living." For example: the niche of a great horned owl in the U.S. would be a nocturnal predator that preys on small birds and mammals. In West Africa there are no great horned owls. Instead, the role of a nocturnal predator is filled by the white-faced owl. Different animals can fill the same niche in different parts of the world.

What would happen if the white-faced owl was introduced to the habitat of the great horned owl? The two species would compete for the same food. Most likely, the strongest would survive.

There have been many species of animals that have been introduced to a new habitat. When that happens, the balance of that environment and the relationships of all the animals in that area are affected in some way.

Use the puppet show entitled *A Lily Pad Tale* to introduce the concept of niche and the balance of nature. The script can be found at the back of this chapter. The show can be performed by a teacher, or students can present the show to another class.

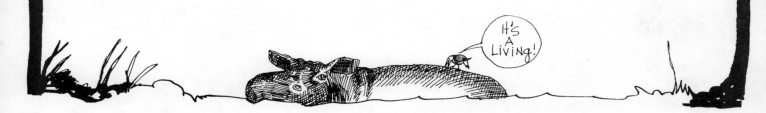

Extinct Is Forever

The passenger pigeon is gone . . . forever.
The Tasmanian wolf is gone . . . forever.
The quagga is gone . . . forever.
The animals are gone . . . forever.
Do you care?

Since 1600, more than 359 species of animals have become extinct.

Exactly what does that mean? An extinct animal no longer exists. That is a very powerful statement. Discuss the idea of extinction with your students and include the following questions:

1. Why should it matter to us whether a species of animal becomes extinct?
2. If a species of animal becomes extinct how are the other living things in that environment affected?
3. Make a list of animal species that have been destroyed by man. Ex: passenger pigeon, dodo bird, plains wolf, eastern elk, etc.
4. How would *you* feel if there were no more elephants (list other creatures).

Many species are gone forever, but there is still time to save the animals left living on this earth. Here is a list of practical things that kids can do to help endangered wildlife.

1. Get to know, love, and respect all living things.
2. Become a member of National Wildlife, the Audubon Society, World Wildlife Fund, and other groups that promote and protect wildlife.
3. Mail a letter to your local city council member, congressman, and the President of the United States in support of all laws that protect wildlife and the environment.
4. Become involved with your local zoo.
5. Conserve natural resources whenever possible. Saving electricity, paper, and water will affect wildlife in a positive way.
6. Boycott products from countries who do not conserve wildlife. Japan, Russia, and Canada are three nations who are currently destroying wildlife for profit.
7. Don't buy products made from animals such as furs, shoes or handbags.

What A dull world without us Dodos.

You would think I might be Missed

Right Whale

Spaces and Places

There are many different animal habitats in the environment. Here are a few: mountains, forests, deserts, grasslands, estuaries, rivers and lakes.

Talk about these places with your children. Has anyone ever visited any of these habitats? How are they different from each other? What kinds of animals might live there?

While it is difficult to take a large group to visit a variety of habitats, it is possible to create several mini-habitats in your own home or classroom. Encourage your children to help you set up an aquarium and a terrarium. The aquarium should contain aquatic organisms such as fish, snails and water plants. The terrarium could house a land-dwelling creature such as a snake, mouse, lizard or guinea pig. Check your local pet store or humane society for more information on pet care. The Happy Herps chapter also has a section on captive care of reptiles.

Review what the animals will need while living in the classroom habitats: food, water, shelter, heat and a clean cage.

Have children observe the two habitats over a period of time. A journal can be kept by each child. Observations on animal behavior, temperature changes and similarities and differences between the two habitats can be recorded daily. Drawings can also be included.

Ask the following questions of your students:

1. What kinds of differences did you notice between the animals living in the aquatic environment and the animals living in the terrestrial environment?

2. Did all the animals eat the same food and in the same manner?

3. Did the creatures move around the habitat? How did they move? Were certain areas preferred over others?

4. Did any of the animals die? If so, what kinds of changes did you observe?

To reinforce what is learned during this activity, take a trip to observe the animal environments at the zoo.

Save That Species

The concept of an endangered species is a vital part of environmental education. It is important for both children and adults to develop an understanding of why a certain species can become threatened or endangered and what they can do to prevent this from happening. The game that follows presents children with situations that endangered animals face during their struggle for existence. Those playing the game must also work to keep the resources necessary for their "existence."

Divide children into teams, and have each team pick the endangered animal they will represent. Each team is then given the same number of resource cards. These cards are either lost or gained according to the team's ability to complete a certain task. Tasks can include math problems, spelling words, geography questions, etc.

Begin the game by asking each team the same question. They must write their answers down and present them to you. A correct answer gives their animal another resource card, an incorrect answer takes away resources. Any team with less than five cards receives a red endangered animal sign and must keep it until they can build up their resources and gain nonthreatened status. The game can continue for a specific period of time. The team with the most resources at the end of the game is the winner.

Another adaptation to this game is to have teams trade resource cards. Animals cannot live with just food so a team can trade food cards for water or habitat cards. This trading is done instead of receiving another card. The winner in this game is the team with the best balance of resources.

Suggestions for resource cards: one week's supply of food, one day's supply of food, a large water hole, just water left from a recent rain, long rain season has given your habitat more food sources, a game reserve has been set up to preserve your species, your habitat has been improved by a conservation group, or a special study is being done to help preserve your species.

Clues and Claws

One of the most exciting experiences is to observe an animal in its native habitat. Sometimes you do not have to see an animal to know that it has been in the area. Here are some clues that animals leave behind that will tell you whether they have passed by.

1. Noise - bird song, stirring in the bushes.
2. Tracks - hoof or paw prints.
3. Leftover food items.
4. Droppings or fecal material.
5. A piece of fur or feathers caught in a tree or on the ground.
6. Empty nests or a hole in the ground (burrow).
7. Shells, skeletons, skin sheddings.
8. Matted grass - maybe where an animal slept or rested for awhile.

Have children look around their school yard or neighborhood for animal signs. Before leaving on any field trip to observe animals, make a list of "do's" and "don'ts."

1. Don't stick your hands in burrows or holes.
2. Do move slowly. Running and yelling will frighten any animal.
3. Remain still if you scare an animal. Allow it to run away. Don't chase it.
4. Do wear sturdy shoes and clothing.
5. Don't forget to take cameras, binoculars and field guides.

Litter Pie

Take an ounce of smog
a dash of glog
a can of rusty nails

A measure of suds
and someone's old duds
found in a garbage pail.

Mix a pound of guck
and a cup of yuck
and drop in a bottle or two.
Add a worn rubber tire
and plenty of mire
then season with someone's old shoe.

OOOH!
A pinch of garbage
buried 'neath the garage
makes this recipe nearly complete

Saute peel of banana
a dirty bandana
and a watch that doesn't tick

Sprinkle on mustard
and yesterday's custard
Oh, dear, you're making me sick!

Pound it and ground it
then stew at one hundred and three
toss it and frost it.....
      But, *please* don't serve it to me!

Suggested Activities:

1. Use this poem to introduce a unit on ecology.
2. Have the children draw pictures of the litter pie ingredients.
3. Take an "ecology walk" to collect litter pie ingredients. Return to the classroom and make litter pie using an old tire box as the bowl.
4. Have a litter pie contest between two groups to see who can collect the most litter around the schoolgrounds area.
5. Begin a class discussion on pollution with this poem. Are we doing a good job of taking care of our earth? When we pollute the water, the earth and the sky, what happens to the wildlife? What can we do to help keep our planet clean?

Cycles

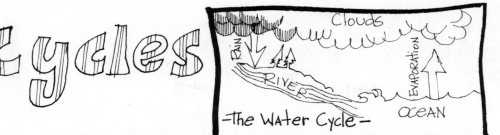

— The Water Cycle —

The environment is made up of a complicated network of living and nonliving cycles. Some of these natural cycles are shown at the end of this activity. Unfortunately, man has the power to disrupt these cycles and upset the balance of the entire natural world. Ask your children to think of ways that man has already disrupted the natural cycles of his environment. What will happen if we continue to destroy habitats, pollute the air and water, and cause more animals to become extinct? How will this affect the balance of the ecosystem?

Explore this topic further by trying the following activity:

Introduce the concept of natural cycles by performing a shadow puppet show. Patterns for the butterfly cycle are found at the end of the Environmental Encounters chapter and general instructions are given here. Shadow puppets can be made by cutting simple shapes out of black poster board. Construct the handle by taping a plastic straw to the back of each puppet. Make the shadow stage out of a cardboard box. Cut out a large opening and stretch white material tightly across the opening to make the shadow screen. Place a light up above and behind the back side of the screen. Point it downward so that it shines directly on the screen and you are ready for your shadow puppet show.

SIMPLIFIED WATER CYCLE

1. This cycle begins with water in a lake, a stream or an ocean.
2. When heated, the water evaporates and becomes part of a cloud.
3. When cooled, the water will fall to the ground as rain, sleet, hail or snow.
4. Raindrops or snowflakes run together to form a puddle, stream, lake or river.

BLACK POSTER BOARD

TAPE

FIGURE

STRAW

TAPE

SIDE VIEW

PLASTIC STRAW

SIMPLIFIED PLANT CYCLE

1. This cycle begins with an apple. Plant the seeds inside the apple.
2. The seeds grow into a tree.
3. The tree will flower.
4. The flower is fertilized.
5. A new apple is formed.
6. When ripe, the new seeds are ready to begin the cycle again.

Cycles Page 2

SIMPLIFIED INSECT CYCLE

1. An egg is laid.
2. A caterpillar hatches.
3. The caterpillar eats and begins to grow.
4. After it stops growing, the caterpillar spins a cocoon.
5. Inside the cocoon the caterpillar changes into a pupae and then into the adult form--a butterfly.
6. The butterfly emerges, mates and lays eggs to begin the cycle all over again.

SIMPLIFIED LIFE CYCLE

Plants and animals are made up of elements such as carbon, caldum and others.

1. A plant or animal dies and begins to decompose.
2. Decomposers such as bacteria break down the dead animal or plant so that it is returned to the soil.
3. Plants use the elements in the soil from the dead plant or animal to help them grow.
4. Animals eat the plants and ingest the elements carbon and calcium.
5. When the animals die, the cycle begins again.

SIMPLIFIED FROG CYCLE

1. An egg is laid.
2. A pollywog hatches.
3. The pollywog eats and grows.
4. The pollywog turns into a frog.
5. The frog matures, mates and lays eggs to begin the cycle all over again.

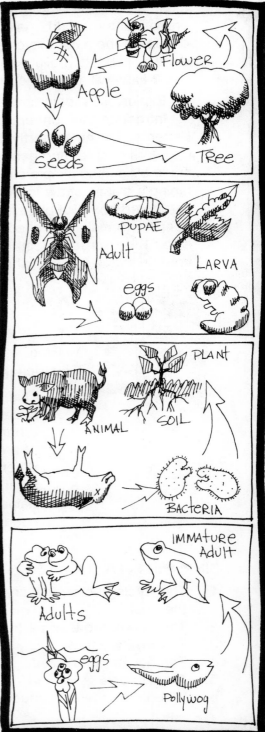

A Lily Pad Tale

The scene opens with two frogs, a turtle and a snake talking about what a good life they live. They are happy because they have plenty of food to eat and a lot of space to move in. Suddenly as they talk, they hear a noise. They all duck down underneath the stage. Human voices are heard. Two large feet walk on stage.

Boy: "I'm tired of this frog. Besides, my mother said I can't keep it anymore. Oh well, this looks like a good place for a frog to live. I'll just leave it here. Good-bye frog."

A splash is heard and a giant bullfrog appears on stage.

Bullfrog: "Jug-O'-rum, Jug-O'-rum. I'm hungry!"

A fly buzzes by and he eats it. A fish swims by and he eats it. As he is swallowing his last bite of fish, a tortoise walks onto the stage. The bullfrog gives him a big shove.

Bullfrog: "Hey, watch out! This is my spot. I was here first! Boy of all the nerve. Trying to steal my hunting territory."

Tortoise: "What's the idea! I was just out for a walk. Why did you shove me? Who are you anyway? You don't look like any frog I've ever seen before."

Bullfrog: "You'd better watch out for me, gramps! This is my spot."

Tortoise: "By my grandfather's shell, I'll never understand this younger generation. Well, I never. Can you belive this disrespect?"

The tortoise exits offstage. Bullfrog begins to look for something else to eat. A small green frog enters from the other side of the stage.

Green Frog: "Ribot, Ribot. Who are you? You don't belong here!"

Bullfrog: "I'm Buford Bullfrog and I'm hungry!"

Green Frog: "How did you get here?"

Bullfrog: "I used to live with a boy, but his mother didn't want him to keep me so he brought me to this nice pond. Say, have you got anything good to eat?"

Green Frog: "That's not fair! He should not have brought you to this pond. Bullfrogs don't live here!"

Bullfrog reaches over and nibbles the other frog's arm.

Bullfrog: "Hmmm, you taste pretty good!"

The other frog gives a cry and beats a hasty retreat.

Bullfrog: "Boy, I sure am hungry! I think I'll go find something to eat. Jug-O'-rum, Jug-O'-rum."

A Lily Pad Tale ... Page 2

It is the next day. The sun has risen over the pond and whispers are heard.

Tortoise: "Is he there?"

Green Frog: "I don't know."

Tortoise: "Go up and take a look."

The lily pad moves. Frog's head appears under the lily pad. He carefully looks around and calls to the others.

Green Frog: "I think it's all right now. I don't see him anywhere."

Slowly the other animals stick their heads up, too--tortoise, diamondback rattler, frog and fish.

Girl Frog: "I'm sure glad that fat ugly frog isn't around."

Green Frog: "I would hate to meet him under a dark lily pad."

Rattlesnake: "SSSSSSSSSS So you know that he tried to eat me! That slimy supercilious sorry frog!!"

He rattles his tail.

Girl Frog: "Watch it!"

Tortoise: "Why...do you know he tried to push me down! The nerve of that big bully!!!"

Green Frog: (In a frightened voice.) "He took a nibble of my arm. I don't feel comfortable around here anymore!"

Girl Frog: "I hear there is a nice marsh over on the other side of the valley. Maybe we should go there!"

Green Frog: "I sure would feel safer."

Snake: "SSSSSSS I shall think seriously before I hunt around this pond again!"

The snake exits.

Tortoise: "I guess you are all right. This place isn't the same anymore, ever since that bullfrog came along. Why, do you know that I saw another one on the other side of the pond while I was taking a walk this morning."

Green Frog: "Before you know it, there will be so many bullfrogs that there won't be room for any of the rest of us!"

Girl Frog: "I think we all should go away!"

They all start to walk sadly off the stage.

Green Frog: "I'm going to miss this old pond."

Bullfrog walks on stage as everyone is leaving. He looks around.

Bullfrog: "Hi! Yoo Hoo! Where is everyone going? I'm hungry. Jug-O'-rum, Jug-O'-rum."

He hops off the stage.

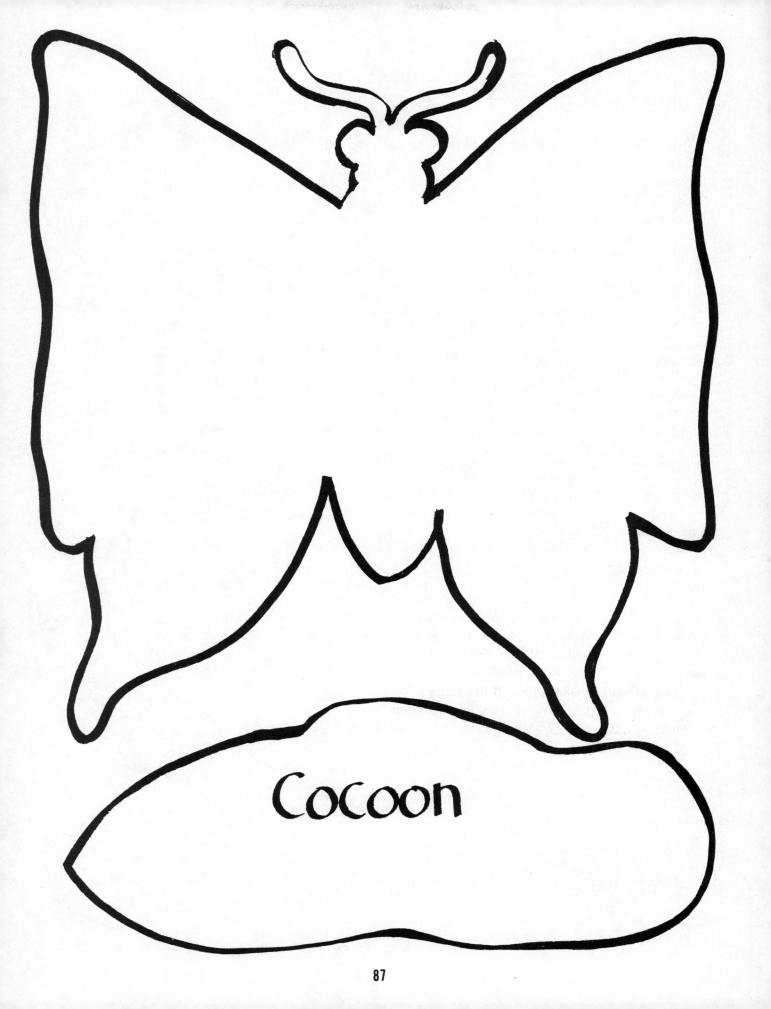

Cocoon

egg

Attach with PAPER Fastener

SMALL Caterpillar

Repeat LeAf Pattern MANY Times

ZOO IT

Blunt, Willfrid, *The Ark in the Park,* Hamish Hamilton, Ltd.
Buchenholz, Bruce, *Doctor in the Zoo,* Viking Press.
Burton, Maurice and Jane, *World Encyclopedia of Animals,* Octopus Books.
Cornell, Joseph Bharat, *Sharing Nature with Children,* Ananda Publications.
Lane, Frank, *Zoo Animals,* Crescent.
Taylor, David, *Zoo Vet,* J.B. Lippincott.
Time-Life, *Zoo Animals,* Time-Life Books.
Time-Life, *Life in Zoos and Preserves,* Time-Life Books.
International Zoo Yearbooks, Zoological Society of London, Regent's Park, London.

MAMMALS

Carrington, Richard, *The Mammals,* Time-Life Books.
Mammals, Golden Nature Guide, Golden Press.
National Geographic, *Book of Mammals,* Vol. I and II, National Geographic Society.
Time-Life, *Elephants and Other Land Giants,* Time-Life Books.

BIRDS

Amon, Aline, *Roadrunners and Other Cuckoos,* Atheneum.
Graham, Ada and Frank, *Falcon Flight,* Delacorte Press.
Henley, Karyn, *Hatch,* Carolrhoda Books.
Hopf, Alice L., *Biography of a Snowy Owl,* Delcorte Press.
Lenga, Rosalind, *The Amazing Fact Book of Birds,* A & P Books.
Peterson, Roger Tory, *The Birds,* Time-Life Books.
Tenaza, Richard, *Penguins,* Franklin Watts.

REPTILES

Bentley, William, *The Alligators Book: 60 Questions and Answers,* Walker.
Carr, Archie, *The Reptiles,* Time-Life Books.
Covenner, Barbara, *A Snake Lover's Diary,* Young Scott Books.
Fichter, George S., *Snakes Around the World,* Franklin Watts.
Hartman, Jane E., *Looking at Lizards,* Holiday House.
Horndow, Leonora and Arthur, *Reptiles Do the Strangest Things,* Random House.
Pringle, Laurence, *Dinosaurs and People,* Harcourt Brace.
Schmidt, Karl P., and Inger, Robert F., *Living Reptiles of the World,* Hanover House.

CONSERVATION/ECOLOGY

Allen, Thomas B., *Vanishing Wildlife of North America,* National Geographic Society.
Anderson, Margaret, *Exploring City Trees and the Need for Urban Forests,* McGraw-Hill.
Burt, Olive W., *Rescued! America's Endangered Wildlife on the Comeback Trail.*

Birds, Beasts, Bugs, and Bigger Fishes, Pete Seeger, Folkway Records.
The Brook, Peter Kilham and Alfred L. Hawkes, Droll Yankees Inc., Millroad, Foster, R.I.
Learning Basic Skills Through Music, Hap Palmer, Educational Activities, Inc.
More Nature Songs, Marais and Miranda, Science Materials Center, Motivation Records.
Nature Songs, Marais and Miranda, Science Materials Center, Motivation Records.
Peter, Paul and Mommy, Peter, Paul, and Mary, Warner Brothers Records.
Spin, Spider, Spin, Marcia Berman and Patty Zeitlin, Educational Activities, Inc.
Songs of Nature and the Environment, Gerry Axecrod and Robert Macklin, Folkway Records.

Agency Contacts Teacher Resources

Animal Protection Institute of America, P.O. Box 22505, Sacramento, CA 95822
Center for Action on Endangered Species, 175 West Main Street, Ayer, MA 01432. Fact sheets about specific endangered animals.
The Humane Society of the United States, 2100 L Street N.W., Washington, D.C. 20037. Send for their publications list. They have a wide variety of teacher resources on animals.
Office of Endangered Species, U.S. Fish and Wildlife Service, Department of the Interior, Washington, D.C. 20240. Lists of endangered species.
National Audubon Society, Educational Services, 950 Third Ave., New York, NY 10022. Ask for the Greenbox - box of activity cards on the environment.
National Wildlife Federation, 1412 16th St. N.W., Washington, D.C. 20036. Ask for their Discovery Units or for the packet of reprints from the *Ranger Rick Magazine.* They also have a list of their current publications.
Reynolds Metals Company, Recycling Public Relations Manager, Box 27003, Richmond, VA 23261. Ask for the unit called Reynolds Aluminum Presents Michael.
Sierra Club, Information Services, 530 Bush Street, San Francisco, CA 94108 Send for a list of literature and teaching materials on different environmental topics.
Standard Brands Educational Service, Box 2695, Grand Central Station, New York, NY 10017. Ask for Mr. Peanuts Guide to Ecology.

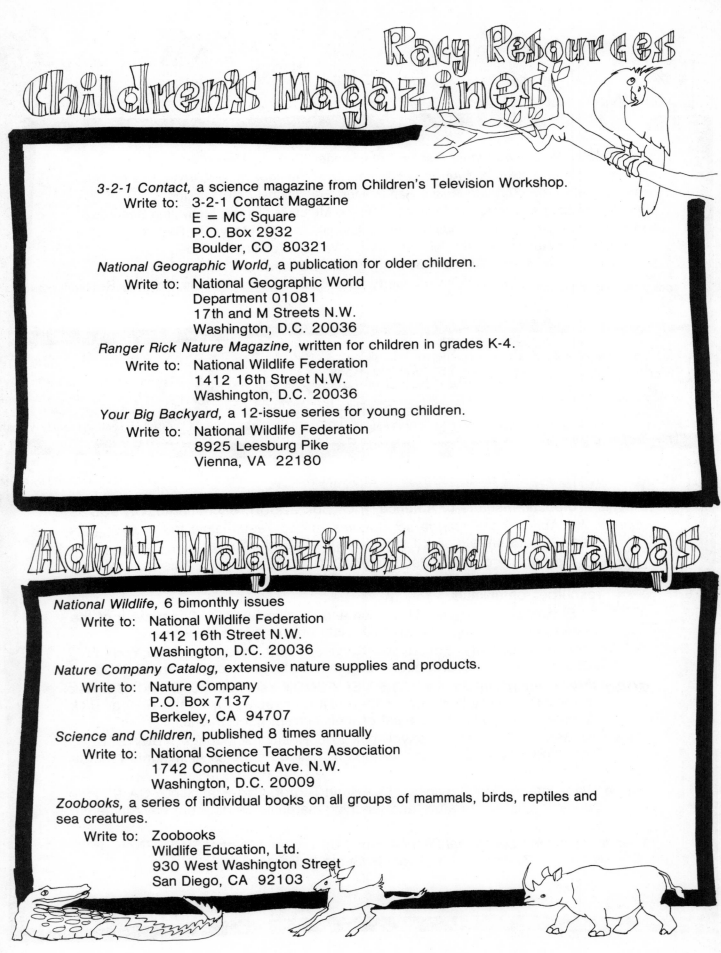

Children's Magazines

3-2-1 Contact, a science magazine from Children's Television Workshop.

Write to: 3-2-1 Contact Magazine
E = MC Square
P.O. Box 2932
Boulder, CO 80321

National Geographic World, a publication for older children.

Write to: National Geographic World
Department 01081
17th and M Streets N.W.
Washington, D.C. 20036

Ranger Rick Nature Magazine, written for children in grades K-4.

Write to: National Wildlife Federation
1412 16th Street N.W.
Washington, D.C. 20036

Your Big Backyard, a 12-issue series for young children.

Write to: National Wildlife Federation
8925 Leesburg Pike
Vienna, VA 22180

Adult Magazines and Catalogs

National Wildlife, 6 bimonthly issues

Write to: National Wildlife Federation
1412 16th Street N.W.
Washington, D.C. 20036

Nature Company Catalog, extensive nature supplies and products.

Write to: Nature Company
P.O. Box 7137
Berkeley, CA 94707

Science and Children, published 8 times annually

Write to: National Science Teachers Association
1742 Connecticut Ave. N.W.
Washington, D.C. 20009

Zoobooks, a series of individual books on all groups of mammals, birds, reptiles and sea creatures.

Write to: Zoobooks
Wildlife Education, Ltd.
930 West Washington Street
San Diego, CA 92103